ADVANCED PRAIS

"As the former director of the Office of National Drug Control Policy, I am well aware that drug trafficking organizations are using America's public lands to cultivate marijuana and are protecting their drug crops with dangerous booby traps. In *War in the Woods*, Lt. John Nores Jr. and James Swan describe in riveting detail the perils faced by brave law enforcement officers across America in confronting drug traffickers on our nation's public lands. This is a compelling read that illuminates the dark side of criminal marijuana cultivation."

—GENERAL BARRY MCCAFFREY, RETIRED,
FORMER DIRECTOR OF THE OFFICE OF NATIONAL
DRUG CONTROL POLICY UNDER PRESIDENT BILL CLINTON

"*War in the Woods* brings to light the dangers and environmental devastation wreaked by illegal marijuana operations on public lands and puts you in the middle of the action as the 'Thin Green Line,' California's Fish and Game Wardens, fight bravely to protect our citizens and our fragile natural places."

—JARED HUFFMAN, CHAIR,
CALIFORNIA ASSEMBLY WATER, PARKS AND WILDLIFE COMMITTEE

"*War in the Woods* tells a fascinating if little known story about how California game wardens are involved with other federal and local policing agencies in cracking down on illegal marijuana farms in California's valuable wilderness. It makes sense to involve game wardens in such interagency teams. Few police officers have the woodsman skills and knowledge of the local terrain necessary to conduct arrests in wilderness areas, but game wardens do. . . . If you like action, you'll love reading these stories. The stories are fast-paced, fascinating, and demonstrate just how dangerous and violent clandestine marijuana gardeners can be."

—GARY MAUSER, PROFESSOR EMERITUS,
INSTITUTE FOR CANADIAN URBAN RESEARCH STUDIES,
SIMON FRASER UNIVERSITY

"A terrifying, fascinating book. Not only is it a heart-racing, adrenaline-pumping page-turner, but it will leave you trembling with rage at how *your* land and *your* water and *your* resources are being stolen and despoiled by drug dealers who are perfectly willing to take your life too, if you go into the woods. Kudos to the extraordinarily courageous game wardens for their work, and to James Swan for his chronicle of their efforts."

—JAMESON PARKER,
WRITER AND ACTOR (*SIMON AND SIMON*)

"Eradicating illegal pot groves on our public lands is not for the faint of heart or the badge-wearing political types looking for a pat on the back. Read *War in the Woods*, and you will begin to truly appreciate game wardens, the rare and endangered species of brave men and women doing a thankless job they know matters."

—MARSHALL TEAGUE, ACTOR
(*ARMAGEDDON*, *AMERICAN HEIRESS*, AND *ROAD HOUSE*)

"In nearly four decades of covering breaking news around the world, I've seen my share of hard men preparing to go into harm's way. My blood started pumping when I began reading *War in the Woods*. The descriptions of tactical squads suiting up and checking the gear of their brother officers is the kind of action that prefaces mortal combat. The realization that these men were preparing for combat with invaders of our national forests, sometimes only a few hundred yards from unsuspecting Americans going about their daily lives, made my blood run cold.

For three days in 480 B.C., 300 Spartans held off the entire Persian army at Thermopylae and became history's most-cited example of the advantages of training, equipment, and knowledge of the terrain to become a symbol of courage against overwhelming odds. Today, only 200 California Fish and Game Wardens are fighting to protect America's public lands from drug dealers looking for their share of the estimated $38.5 billion dollar marijuana business. Today, they're California's Spartans, and *War in the Woods* tells their story—in their words."

—JIM SHEPHERD,
EDITOR/PUBLISHER,
THE OUTDOOR WIRE

WAR IN THE WOODS

COMBATING
THE MARIJUANA CARTELS ON
AMERICA'S PUBLIC LANDS

Lt. John Nores Jr., California Department of Fish and Game,
with James A. Swan, PhD

LYONS PRESS
GUILFORD, CONNECTICUT

An imprint of Globe Pequot Press

Lyons Press is an imprint of Globe Pequot Press.

All photos are courtesy of the author.

Text design: Sheryl P. Kober

Library of Congress Cataloging-in-Publication Data
Nores, John.
  War in the woods : combating marijuana cartels on America's public lands / John Nores Jr. and James A. Swan.
    p. cm.
  ISBN 978-1-59921-930-1
  1. Marijuana—California. 2. Public lands—California. 3. Drug control—California. 4. Drug traffic—California. I. Swan, James A. II. Title.
  HV5822.M3N67 2010
  363.4509794—dc22
                                2010029109

Printed in the United States of America
10 9 8 7 6 5 4 3 2 1

DEDICATION

For my fellow operators on the Santa Clara County Marijuana Eradication Team: It is an honor and pleasure to work with all of you. I hope you find the following pages on our team's growth, missions, and challenges as rewarding to read as they were for me to write.

For Dale Anne: I appreciate your guidance, support, advice, and friendship in the years we were blessed to have you with us. Thank you for giving us four siblings the tools you had in a very small toolbox to keep the wolf pack together and to realize our dreams. We love you and pray that you rest in peace.

For Charlotte Dawn: Thank you for your support, friendship, and enthusiasm. You inspire me to be more than I am.

For my fellow California game wardens: It is an honor to work beside the finest conservation officers anywhere. I appreciate your dedication and sacrifice to be part of the Department of Fish and Game's Thin Green Line of game wardens and to tirelessly protect our state's wildlife resources.

CONTENTS

FOREWORD

Cannabis, hash, Acapulco gold, ganja, kef, Panama red, northern lights, white widow, weed, Mary Jane, reefer, roach, giggleweed, marijuana, pot, dope, joint, Buddha grass—whatever you call it, *Cannabis sativa* has been used for thousands of years all around the world. Fully 4 percent of the world's population today regularly uses this six-foot-tall annual psychoactive herb for medicinal, spiritual, and recreational purposes whether it's legal or not.

In the United States it is illegal to grow or possess cannabis without special medical and legal permission. Fourteen states now have medical marijuana laws, and others have them in progress. Regardless of whether it's legit or not, growing and selling marijuana is worth as much as $35.8 billion a year in the United States, exceeding the combined value of crops such as corn ($23.3 billion) and wheat ($7.5 billion). It is the number one cash crop of the United States, and possibly the world.

I went to college in the 1960s at the University of Michigan and played rock and folk music. You can guess whether I inhaled or not.

Forty years ago "pot" was grown by long-haired, back-to-nature hippies, and bales of "weed" were smuggled across the border and into the United States from Central America. With toughened border crossing controls and a beefed-up Department of Homeland Security, today's marijuana is more often being cultivated within the boundaries of the United States and Canada, and hippie marijuana farmers are a relatively rare species.

While some growers use greenhouses, plots tucked in cornfields, underground bunkers, and hydroponics, the biggest illegal gardens are located on local, state, and federal parks and wildlands. Bad dudes—organized crime syndicates, primarily Mexican drug cartels—cultivate these gardens. Unlike the flower children pot growers of the 1960s and 1970s, drug cartel–sponsored marijuana farmers are well armed and not afraid to protect themselves and their gardens with firepower and booby traps.

Like a lot of people, I had read in the newspapers about illicit marijuana gardens on wildland, as far back as the mid-1990s. But, I had never seen it firsthand until I produced a documentary film about California's Fish and Game Wardens. The wardens invited me and my son to ride along and film a marijuana garden bust in Foothills Park in Palo Alto, California, just a few miles west of Stanford University Stadium in 2008.

We met the team at dawn at a commuter parking lot near I-680 and Page Mill Road—a dozen men from three different agencies dressed in tactical camouflage gear gathered near the Starbuck's latte-sipping commuters who were waiting for a bus. On cue from a radio dispatcher, everyone hopped in their trucks and drove west in a caravan along Page Mill Road. A couple of miles later the procession turned onto a gravel side road that snaked into Foothills Park: a large natural area with live oak and laurel groves and steep gullies filled with the kind of thick chaparal brush that dry season fires love to devour. Our base camp was on a hill above the garden, which had been spotted from the air by helicopter. Shortly, California Fish and Game warden Lt. John Nores and the other members of his team came together in a circle, like a football team assembling before a big game.

The command leader went over the day's plan as a helicopter approached. As it landed nearby, the meeting ended. Team members who were going into the garden checked their rifles and pistols and tactical gear and made ready for action.

The ground crew attached a 150-foot-long steel wire to the helicopter. John and another warden stepped up and were strapped into the harness used to extract people by helicopter, which was at the end of the wire. They signaled with a wave, and slowly the whirlybird rose 150 feet off the ground, pulling the two wardens into the air.

After the wardens were about 300 feet above the ground, the helicopter headed off horizontally at about 70 mph—"short-hauling" into the grove. What a way to commute to work! To keep from being twirled around under the speeding helicopter, each warden extended one arm outward to break the spin, while the other hand clutched the wire with an iron grip. The team had to be high enough while en route to pass over high-tension electrical wires.

This garden was about a half a mile away down a steep brushy canyon. The short-haul made the wardens' approach quicker, and it enabled them to pass over a thicket of poison oak that surrounded the garden. Pot growers like to use poison oak patches for defending their gardens; it tends to keep people away.

This was a tense time. Hanging on a rope from a helicopter, the men were totally exposed to ground fire, and while they might be able to shoot back, any accuracy while hanging there with one hand free would be nearly impossible. The helicopter itself represented an even bigger target. Some have been shot in such raids.

In groups of two, the rest of the team short-hauled out. We anxiously waited at the command center while the garden was cleared and reports came in on the radio. "The growers have fled," was the message that came back over the radio.

Finally, the "All Clear" message came through, and my son and I boarded the helicopter with our cameras. (No, we did not short-haul.)

When the pilot said that we had reached the space above ground zero, I looked down and saw a green carpet of chaparral interspersed with live oaks. "Where's the garden? I don't see any-thing," I said.

We came to a stationary position, and the pilot said, "Watch." He slowly descended, lowering the short-haul line to pick up a bale of freshly cut plants. As the rotor wash began to push down the overstory of manzanita and mesquite, suddenly an understory of bright green plants began to appear. As the marijuana plants were pushed down, what emerged was a spider web of black plastic irri-gation lines woven among the grove of six-foot-tall plants, as well as a jumble of other materials that had been painted in camouflage green and brown to avoid detection from the air. Team members in camo emerged from the bushes and hung a net full of plants on the end of the short-haul line.

With a bundle of marijuana about the size of two bales of straw attached to the short-haul line, the helicopter rose. This time, we took a slightly different route, over Page Mill Road. The sharp-eyed pilot said that he saw something suspicious.

He dropped us off and went back for a closer look.

When John's team came back to base camp on short-hauls a couple of hours later, they sat down to rest and eat as the crew loaded 10,000 plants into a trailer. Minutes later, the helicopter landed, and the team leader walked over to tell the men they were not finished. A closer inspection had revealed another garden less than a mile away and bigger than the one they had just cleared. "It's located within 50 yards of heavily traveled Page Mill Road and less than 100 yards from some upscale houses," the team leader reported.

We picked up and moved across Page Mill Road, parking within a quarter mile of this grove. This time some of the team short-hauled in quickly to try to catch sight of the growers from the air, while another group came in on foot. Again, the gardeners had disappeared likes snakes in tall grass.

When the "All Clear" came through, my son and I were allowed to walk into the garden with an armed escort—John Nores and an M14. We did not go more than 50 yards from the stream of commuters passing along Page Mill Road through a jumble of brush 8 to 10 feet tall, when we came to a 3-foot-tall fence of chicken wire woven through the brush. John said this was the perimeter of the garden. Every few feet along the wire fence were boxes of d-Con baits and traps to keep out rabbits and mice.

As we followed John into the garden, we stayed right behind him and in his tracks, for as he explained, booby traps were sometimes placed around these gardens—trip wires, bear traps, spikes on boards hidden in the grass, and even pits with spikes at the bottom that someone, including an unsuspecting hiker or hunter, could fall into.

Inside the rabbit-proof fence, the understory had been neatly cleared away, and wherever you looked there was a well-tended crop of bright green 6-foot-tall marijuana plants hidden under the overstory of taller bushes and trees. Each plant was linked to a line from a drip irrigation system that ended with an emitter and a timer at the base of the plant.

Nearby, several bags of fertilizer were covered with brush.

As we passed team members cutting plants with machetes, John led us to the growers camp—two cots covered with Army surplus camouflage netting, a propane stove, ice chest, some empty and full cans of food, and several 55-gallon drums painted dull green. These held the water that was fed to the plants through the irrigation system. It appeared that the growers, were stealing water at night from nearby homes to keep the barrels filled. I cannot imagine how they got the drums in there—it was hard enough to just walk in through brush carrying nothing.

Not far from the cots was an Army surplus ammo box and a couple of spent cartridges; a chilling find. Nearby, strips of venison jerky were hanging in a tree to dry. The deer's carcass was found in the brush outside the rabbit fence. Was that deer shot, or had it been caught in a pitfall or a bear trap? People in the nearby homes would have heard a gunshot.

All this was within 100 yards of homes with kids playing games and people sitting on their front porches enjoying margaritas as the sun went down.

In that one day John and his team removed about 30,000 marijuana plants worth millions of bucks on the street where weed would sell for anywhere from $1,500 to $6,000 a pound, depending on the quality.

In many ways these illicit grow operations are like terrorist cells. The individual gardeners report to one person. Each gardener does not necessarily know about others nearby. Sometimes rival growers do engage in territorial warfare, but we don't hear about this too much, because the law of the woods for these folks is to follow the three S's—shoot, shovel, and shut up.

I came away from seeing this clandestine agricultural operation realizing that armed enemy combatants who have a license to kill anyone who stumbles into their gardens are infiltrating our public lands. That day, we had entered a war zone.

More than half of all the illegal marijuana grown in North America today is cultivated on such clandestine plots on wildlands—state and national parks, national forests, wildlife reserves, etc. Illegal marijuana gardens can be found from coast to coast and from the Mexican border up to Alaska. They are everywhere, but nowhere does that industry flourish more than in California, whose illegal crop is estimated to be worth $14 billion a year.

It is estimated that more than 5,000 people are currently employed in the illegal marijuana industry in California. In some counties, growing illegal marijuana is the biggest economic industry, yet the only taxes collected are from sales of agricultural supplies for the growers, and our tax dollars support these public lands and the men and women who protect them.

John's eradication team is one of several, and they all could use a lot more help. More than five million marijuana plants were eradicated from California public wildlands in 2008. The number of marijuana plants confiscated on public land in California grew from 40 percent to 75 percent of total seizures between 2001 and 2007, according to the Campaign Against Marijuana Planting (CAMP), a multi-agency law enforcement task force. In 2009 the number of plants eradicated by CAMP set a new record.

Put aside your opinions on whether you think marijuana should be legal for a moment and consider how rogue marijuana gardens wreak havoc on the land and wildlife, threaten the safety of anyone venturing into the woods, fuel a street-gang-run drug trade, and return no tax dollars to the community.

In addition to running an illicit drug business using armed growers, these illegal gardeners do horrendous damage to the environment—diverting streams, poisoning land and water with toxic pesticides and fertilizers, removing native vegetation, causing erosion and landslides, and poaching wild animals for food. Once the growing season begins in April, growers typically move in and live 24/7 in the groves until the harvest is finished in late October. Booby traps including bear traps, snares, pitfalls, trip wires, and dead falls are not uncommon. The growers are heavily armed, with orders to protect their groves with deadly force. Some growers intercepted in 2009 said they have begun building bunkers and are arming themselves with sniper rifles. Agents from the U.S. Drug Enforcement Administration (DEA) and the Bureau of Alcohol, Tobacco, Firearms, and Explosives (BATF) have intercepted people with such arms who said they were on the way to gardens.

Because these rogue gardens harm wildlife and are located on public wildlands, the war on marijuana in state and national parks, forests, and wildlife refuges is often spearheaded by game wardens, perhaps the least known, least understood, and least respected of all law enforcement officers. Most people think of game wardens as people like dogcatchers who drive around checking hunters and fishermen to see if they have exceeded the number and size limits of legal fish and game, or maybe if they poached an extra squirrel.

Did you know that game wardens enforce the widest range of laws of any state or local law enforcement officer, and that being a game warden is one of the most dangerous of all law enforcement jobs? In the following pages you will understand why that is true as you enter a world that is more like jungle warfare than policing a beat.

Lt. John Nores is one of the game wardens on the front line; part of a courageous interagency team that works mostly alone but also collaborates with other allied agency task force teams and CAMP.

In California, as is the case elsewhere in the United States and Canada, game wardens have increasingly become involved with combating illegal gardens because they are often the only law enforcement agents who patrol remote areas where groves are cultivated, and the wardens are the most woods-wise of any law enforcement officers. Growers have come to hate game wardens with a passion. The DEA has intercepted messages from Mexican drug cartels telling their growers to shoot on sight any wardens they see and that a bounty will be paid for every warden killed. The war in the woods over marijuana is one more reason why being a game warden has become as dangerous as being a DEA agent.

All across North America, state and federal game wardens are becoming involved in combating illegal drugs developed in marijuana groves and meth labs on wildlands. In California the problem is especially acute not only because of the proximity to Mexico and the favorable climate, but because California has the fewest wardens per capita in the United States. California currently has about 200 wardens in the field for 38 million people, resulting in a $100-million-a-year black market in illegal wildlife trafficking as well as skyrocketing drug manufacturing on wildlands. California's Department of Fish and Game Law Enforcement Chief Nancy Foley believes that she needs 3,000 wardens to handle the state's needs, and 7,000 would not be too many.

You may have read about marijuana busts in national parks. Most news stories cover the facts and maybe include a picture or two. It should upset you that our national natural resource heritage is being trashed and poisoned. But you can't really appreciate the risks involved in trying to protect our wildlands and make them safe unless you have walked, bushwhacked, crawled, run, and short-hauled with the brave men and women who do this every summer as part of their job of protecting natural resources. That's why John Nores and his buddies decided to let you into their world.

This book features tales of actual drug busts by an allied agency Marijuana Eradication Team (MET) on public wildlands told through the eyes of a gutsy game warden on the front line. John's stories paint a dramatic picture of the real dirt, guts, and sometimes blood involved in being on the front line of conservation. The Thin Green Line of game wardens needs your support and respect. You are about to see why.

—James A. Swan
April 2010

INTRODUCTION

Unlike so many of my colleagues in the California Department of
Fish and Game, I, Lt. John Nores Jr., did not know I wanted to be
a game warden at an early age. I was not influenced by interacting
with game wardens as a young outdoorsman like some of my game
warden friends. I do, however, come from a conservation-oriented
family. My father and uncles introduced me to hunting and fishing
sports when I was nine, from which I developed a love and appreciation for the outdoors and a yearning to learn about all the wildlife
of California.

With my father's guidance, I passed my hunter safety exam when
I was nine and began hunting waterfowl with him shortly after that.
During my early teen years I received my first deer-hunting rifle
from my future father-in-law. I spent that summer working off the
cost of that rifle as I was taught how to properly shoot a scoped rifle
and to hand load precision ammunition to get the most accuracy
and stopping power from a particular cartridge, bullet, and rifle
combination. I enjoy weapons. I respect them and understand that
they hold the power of life and death. They are an extension of our
intentions.

You could say I was hooked on nature, so much so that it
became my spiritual touchstone. Every summer weekend, my three
siblings and I (the "wolf pack" as our mom called the four of us)
camped out under our family's two giant pine trees. Early morning
waterfowl and deer hunts throughout California with my dad and
future father-in-law were magical times that later turned into week-

long backpacking trips throughout the remote backcountry regions of Henry W. Coe State Park, the largest state park in northern California, during spring and winter breaks in high school and college.

These trips excited and rewarded me more than any other activity throughout my youth, but when it came to college and looking at a future career, I chose to follow in an uncle's very successful footsteps and pursue a career in civil engineering. So in 1986, following my high school graduation, I enrolled in a civil engineering program at San José State University and banked on my career destiny that I set in motion. Or so I thought.

And then the best thing happened. I met a game warden. Perhaps it was fate or a little influence from the good Lord above, but it happened at the best time in my life to make a change.

While on winter break from college, I was horse packing with my good friend and future brother-in-law, Jeff, in the backcountry of Henry W. Coe State Park. After riding through a downpour for an entire day and stopping late that night, we set up camp at a remote lake and nearly froze during the night. We made a fire the next morning to avoid hypothermia and dry out our gear. While warming up by the fire, I looked up and noticed a green four-wheel-drive truck crawling slowly down a steep fire road above our camp. Within a few minutes a game warden was talking with us as we sat around the fire.

Although I didn't know it at the time, he was subtly checking us out for poaching activity and other violations in our camp. Finding none, he chose to stay and talk for a while and that's when the light bulb turned on for me. I started bombarding him with questions. Two long and generous hours later he was finally leaving our camp, and I knew what I wanted to do with my life. Over the next six days of that pack trip I made up my mind to leave the engineering program at school and pursue a career as a game warden. Getting paid to patrol the most beautiful backcountry areas of our county and hunt down and catch poachers was an amazing opportunity to me. While I loved the sport of the chase in general, the thought of chasing and stopping wildlife criminals seemed like the most rewarding hunt of all.

Before that winter break ended, I spoke to an adviser in the criminal justice program at San José State and changed my major before the spring semester started.

In 1990 I graduated with a bachelor's degree and was on the hiring list for a game warden position while waiting for a state-wide hiring freeze to lift in the Department of Fish and Game. I started working part-time as a Juvenile Probation Counselor for delinquent teenagers in juvenile hall and began a graduate program at San José State to obtain a master's degree. I enjoyed working in law, ethics, and justice, but I knew my career goals could never be fully realized unless I could work outdoors protecting our natural resources.

In 1992 that opportunity finally arrived, and I became a cadet at the New Wardens Resource Academy at Napa Valley College in early February. It was a dream come true. I was actually getting paid while in training for my dream job!

That was eighteen years ago, and I have not looked back since. Those years have been truly amazing, exciting, and challenging, and I still feel so rewarded when I catch a hardcore poacher in the act of destroying our wildlife resources.

People ask often ask me why after all these years I am so energetic and passionate about this job and driven to catch bad guys. Two reasons come to mind. The first is the excitement of the hunt and the thrill of the chase. Becoming a hunter of numerous wildlife species at an early age made me realize how much I loved hunting, and that awareness transcended to my ultimate desire to do this job so passionately. My skills of hunting and tracking animals gave me a foundation to track the people who exploit them. Catching a poacher is a challenge, and I like challenges.

The second reason, frankly, is the spirituality of so many aspects of this job. For me, being in the outdoors surrounded by the beauty of our natural resources is calming, uplifting, enlightening, and incredibly motivating. In fact I can meet every challenge I face a little easier if I am spiritually motivated by the outdoors or if I am around wildlife. Whether swimming, biking, or running to train for my next Ironman triathlon; prerunning through the deserts of Baja, Mexico, on an ATV to prepare for the next Baja 1,000 race; or hiking many miles in the snow to find just the right remote, wooded spot to place a deer hunting blind, I have more energy, motivation, and a more rewarding feeling because I can do all of these activities in the wild.

Here's an example. As I write this I'm in a Montana wilderness, sitting in a ground blind in a cold, snow-covered forest meadow 10 miles from the nearest person, waiting for a monster whitetail buck deer to show up so I can fill my deer tag. Just being out in this remote, wooded venue recharges my batteries regardless of what shows up or not.

Why risk my neck to chase marijuana growers? Because the rewards are huge, not financially but from the standpoint of justice. These cultivation sites, and the dangerous men destroying our wildlife resources within them, care not a bit about conservation or enjoying the wilds. Their motivation is simple—greed. And they are deadly serious about it. They are destroying what means so much to me and the rest of the team, other members of the public, and future generations of outdoor enthusiasts. Protecting nature helps us all and the entire ecosystem that enables the natural world to thrive.

Yeah, it's dangerous. Darn dangerous, but above and beyond the adrenalin rush, the process of catching and stopping these brazen natural resource criminals makes this hunt the most dangerous, challenging, and rewarding of them all—maybe a little like what Ernest Hemingway once said: "Certainly there is no hunting like the hunting of man, and those who have hunted armed men long enough and liked it, never care for anything else thereafter."

In 2004, I was the first game warden to join the Santa Clara County Sheriff's Office Marijuana Eradication Team. Up until then, game wardens throughout my region had little involvement in marijuana eradication operations throughout their patrol districts, and little if any influence on environmental crime prosecution, and reclamation and restoration operations. When finding my first large scale cultivation operation (as described in Chapter 1 of this book) and meeting the sheriff's office MET members for the first time, this situation quickly changed. Game wardens were recognized for their tactical skill sets when operating in the woods, as well as their expertise in assessing and investigating the related environmental crimes. An immediate bond and relationship was formed between game wardens and members of the sheriff's office to form the first allied agency MET within Santa Clara County.

Sharing the same public safety concerns, and seeing the egregious environmental destruction in cultivation sites for the first time, engendered a highly effective allied agency partnership with operators from the sheriff's office MET. This partnership would lead to record level eradication, arrest, and environmental restoration and clean up figures over the next five years. This book will highlight some of the most exciting and relevant arrest and eradication missions spanning a five-year period between 2004 and 2009. These missions were pivotal in shaping and defining the MET's tactics, training, and equipment needs over that time period. These stories will also describe the growth and evolution of our special operations team, and the constant change to stay safe, progressive, and professional over that time span and beyond.

To protect the identities of the officers, they are referred to by their call signs, rather than names, throughout this book. Call signs are nicknames developed by other tactical team members that fit the personality or skill set of a particular operator. You'll soon find out why names like "Apache," "Snake," "Markos," "Ranger," "Rails," "Spag," and "Cheetah" are fitting descriptions for the MET members of Santa Clara County.

CHAPTER 1

Palassou Ridge:
The MET Meets for the
First Time

I can learn to persist
 With anything but aiming low.
I can learn to close my eyes
To anything but injustice.

—Rush, "Resist"

The cell phone chimed at 6:00 a.m., waking me up from a much desired sleep. It was a Monday morning in June 2004, and I had had about three precious hours of shut-eye following a long spotlighting patrol for deer poachers the previous night. With game wardens being on call 24/7 throughout their districts, and with no rest for the weary, I reluctantly stretched my stiff back and answered the annoying beast, muttering to myself, "This had better be good."

It was GI, a family friend and private-sector wildlife biologist who works throughout Santa Clara County.

"GI, what's going on? Why are you calling me so damn early?" I grumbled.

"Sorry, Trailblazer, I know you worked late last night, but this is important and strange," he replied.

"What do you mean?"

"Well, you know I'm doing my graduate study up on the Palassou Ridge and monitoring two creeks that are habitat for yellow-legged and red-legged frogs. Yesterday when checking a channel just north of Dexter Canyon, I noticed the creek flow had completely stopped. When I did a quick survey upstream, I didn't see a single frog, fish, or other aquatic species during the entire hike. Something is going on upstream, and it can't be good."

GI explained that the creek flow was normally heavy this time of year, and because the area is so remote he was fearful of a water diversion. If he was right, this diversion would surely kill all fish and aquatic species in the stream channel, including the frogs (which are on the federal and state lists of endangered and threatened species). In addition, this channel fed directly into the headwaters of Coyote Creek, a natural steelhead trout waterway.

I asked GI if he would be available later that day to hike with me into the channel and investigate. We agreed to meet at the gate of the Palassou Ridge property around 8:00 a.m.

Located in south Santa Clara County near Gilroy Hot Springs, the Palassou Ridge contains about 4,000 acres of steep, heavily wooded, rolling hills used in the past as a deer hunting club and cattle ranch. In the mid-1990s the ranch was purchased by the Santa Clara County Open Space Authority for public hiking and enjoyment. Since the land became an Open Space Authority property for future public enjoyment when development funds became available in the future, human presence decreased considerably. With the exception of GI's hiking and crawling around the numerous remote and isolated stream channels and canyons for his research sampling, the canyons were now virtually unchecked. With limited Open Space staff to patrol the area this property was wide open not only to wildlife poaching but to other crimes that damaged environmental resources as well.

Always the eager beaver, GI was waiting in his hiking clothes and with his pack when I arrived at the gate. Experienced in rural field operations from his surveillance of numerous poachers for the Department of Fish and Game in the past, GI was dressed in his military woodland camouflage battle dress uniform (BDU), ready to blend with the wooded environment we would soon be exploring.

Before parking our trucks discreetly near the stone ranch house on the Palassou Ridge property, we discussed our recon plan for the day. We had two options: start at the base of the dewatered drainage and simply hike upstream and uphill until we found the source of the water flow problem, or come in from the top. Dropping into the creek bottom from the ridgeline was preferable. Given the possibility of running into the people in the creek who were responsible for the low water flow, I wanted to have the high ground if we made contact. Moving into a hostile area from above is always a tactical advantage.

GI jumped into my truck, and I drove us slowly up the dirt road that would take us to the top of the ridgeline above the creek. The topography changed from dense brush to open meadows and oak trees as we reached the top of the ridge. I parked under the canopy of a huge oak tree next to a grassy saddle above the creek that descended into the steep canyon. After grabbing our packs, we quietly closed the doors of the truck. For a moment we stood motionless, just taking in the surrounding woods. The peaceful ridgeline was virtually silent except for a few songbirds flying nearby. Being here in this remote place, far above the city of Gilroy in the valley below, was a rush. I charged the firing chamber of my M14 rifle, easing the operating rod forward slowly to keep the loading process as quiet as possible before we moved south and down the hillside toward the creek. You never know what's around the next bush.

The hike into the canyon was steep. Moving quietly downhill was difficult given the dry and crunchy carpet of bay and oak leaves on the ground. The canyon sloped down to the creek, and the sunlight above us started to fade quickly as we descended. By the time we reached the edge of the creek we had descended about a half mile. Across the canyon we could see the steep rock walls of the creek bed. With moss and ferns growing sporadically along the walls of the creek bank, this channel looked more suited to northern California's coastal redwood forests. It was simply pristine and beautiful.

In the lead, I slowly scanned left and right with my rifle as I checked the surrounding creek bank. All was quiet and I detected no movement. Before moving, I looked back at GI and nodded my head up and down. He understood and I slowly climbed down into the creek bottom with him following me.

In the creek bottom we saw several small waterfalls feeding a large natural pool below us. Here the creek was flowing well, keeping the pool below us full of clean, natural runoff water. Scanning the ground, my eyes caught something out of place. At the bottom of the pool I saw a green garden hose that continued downstream and out of view past a bend in the creek about 30 yards ahead of us. As I covered the area with my rifle, I asked GI to take my camera and snap some evidence photos before we continued downstream while I kept scanning for people.

With GI close behind, I moved slowly downstream, stepping on dry rocks to cushion the noise and leave no tracks or other evidence of our presence. What we saw next when rounding the bend was alarming. The garden hose ended in another large pool of water, this one not so pristine. This water hole had been dug out of the creek bed mainly with hand tools. It was lined with black plastic, and there were several black plastic irrigation lines inside the pool and branching out into the surrounding hillsides. The water in the pool looked discolored and had an oily sheen to it. Next to the creek were several empty bags of plant fertilizer, rat poison, and other hazardous products. We had found the reason the downstream flow of this creek had stopped and the explanation for no frog presence in the area. Whoever had built this little reservoir and impounded the creek had mixed poisons directly in the pool and killed everything in the channel for miles below.

On the hillsides above, we could see numerous bright green marijuana plants on both sides of the channel. No more than a foot tall, they had been recently planted. Now we knew why the creek was dry miles below us. Whoever did this was looking at multiple Fish and Game code violations for pollution and stream bed alteration as well as a felony crime of marijuana cultivation.

We moved slowly out of the creek bed and up into the garden site, scanning ahead for growers anywhere near us. We saw no one and quickly checked the plants. We were on the edge of a garden of 2,000 plants that appeared to be one of several that continued downstream as far as the eye could see. With my binoculars I could see a tent, kitchen, and camp area farther downstream. Marijuana plants were everywhere on both sides of the creek bank with an elaborate spiderweb of a plastic irrigation watering system on the ground throughout the garden. Large oak, willow, and cottonwood trees had been chopped down along the creek bank. All the grasses and other riparian vegetation along the bank had also been removed as far as we could see.

All signs pointed to a Mexican drug cartel grow operation. Everything throughout the garden was camouflaged to avoid detection. The water lines, attached drip system, watering buckets, hand tools, pesticide sprayers, and almost anything else on the ground were painted drab olive green. Woodland camouflage tarps covered the entire kitchen, camp, and tent area, making detection from the air impossible.

The creek from where we stood and all the way downstream was completely destroyed. Several man-made pools had scarred the natural course of this pristine stream, and the level of destruction to the creek was appalling. This grow site was huge, sophisticated, and had been in place for several years, operating undetected until now.

I realized we were lucky to find this grow site, judging from the steep banks of the creek and the thick canopy of tree cover above us. If it hadn't been for GI's close monitoring of this area, this operation may have continued for years. Impossible to be seen from the air and unlikely to be hiked by Open Space Authority staff or others given its remote location, finding this site was like finding a needle in a haystack.

Earlier in my career, I assisted in the eradication of a handful of gardens in southern California. Up until this point, I had never seen a grow operation so insidious and environmentally destructive. This was an ecological disaster.

Because the plants had been recently watered, we realized the growers had to be close by. I motioned to GI that it was time to leave. This was the largest and remotest grow site I had ever seen in Santa Clara County, and it was time to exit the danger zone and come up with a game plan to eradicate the garden and restore this pristine waterway.

After taking a few quick evidence photos, I gave GI the hand signal to move back into the creek, and he nodded in agreement. We moved slowly into the creek bed and stopped. As I scanned downstream toward the grow site I noticed movement ahead of us. I froze and whispered to GI, "Movement ahead." I slowly dropped to a knee, and GI followed doing the same. At the top of the creek bank about 30 yards ahead and west of our position was a man dressed in a brown shirt and woodland camouflage pants. This man knew something about field craft and was dressed to blend with his environment. The grower was holding a machete and chopping tree branches, apparently making room for more of his crop. The man stopped chopping and began walking upstream along a trail on the bank of the creek toward our position. GI and I hugged the bank of the creek to stay out of the man's sight while I covered the grower with my rifle. He was one of who knew how many more growers in the garden coming our way, and we were pinned down.

Avoiding detection was paramount. If discovered, we would not be able to return with a bigger team to eradicate the crop and catch the growers on site. Another problem was the fact that GI and I were only a two-man scout team. We were drastically undermanned to eradicate the crop and safely apprehend this man and whomever else was present. Even worse, if this dude with the machete kept closing in on us and we had to make contact, the situation could very easily turn deadly. I was all too familiar with numerous stories of Mexican drug cartel grow operations where the growers were armed with rifles, shotguns, and pistols, as well as knives. And in many cases these men would use them on anyone, especially law enforcement officers, to protect their high-dollar crop.

The grower kept closing the distance between us, looking around and ahead as he walked. As he closed in, our hearts raced and our bodies shook with instant adrenaline dumps. He was 20 yards away and closing, 15 yards, now 10 yards. With my rifle leveled on his chest and my finger ready to press the trigger, just seconds from identifying myself we got a break. The grower stopped just 7 yards ahead of us. He turned his head to the left where the trail continued on into the garden and disappeared. Both of us let out a sigh of relief and waited silently to make sure the grower did not return. I was drenched in sweat. I noticed GI's hands were shaking.

After a few minutes it appeared the man had kept moving. So we moved upstream and into the creek, starting the uphill climb out of the creek bed and up to the truck. As we hiked quietly, I realized that given the layout of the garden, we had likely found our first cartel grow site in Santa Clara County. In an area so remote and difficult to find, my mind reeled at how many more of these illicit garden sites were probably present in my county.

As soon as we had cell phone coverage on the valley floor I called Marko, the supervisor for the Unified Narcotics Enforcement Team (UNET). Working within the California Department of Justice's Bureau of Narcotics Enforcement, UNET is an allied agency task force comprised of officers from several different cities throughout San Benito, Santa Clara, and Monterey Counties. Up to this point in my career, I had not yet met or worked with members of Santa Clara County's MET. Having worked effectively with Marko and his team from the UNET a handful of times in the past, I called him to report our findings.

Marko was excited and immediately began to coordinate his team. Within days, his agents were working with me on a game plan to safely arrest the growers and eradicate the garden.

We waited until the beginning of August, when helicopter teams from the military and the Department of Justice marijuana eradication teams were operational, to complete the mission. By doing so, we had the option of helicopter support for extraction of the marijuana as well as the capability to extract ground team members if needed.

The operations briefing was held the afternoon before the detail. Law enforcement officers from the UNET (San Benito County Sheriff's Office, the California Highway Patrol, and the Hollister, Gilroy, and Morgan Hill Police Departments), the MET (Santa Clara County Sheriff's Office), the Department of Fish and Game, and the California Department of Parks and Recreation were present. This operation was large and incorporated officers from not only the UNET task force and the Santa Clara County MET, but larger state agencies like Fish and Game and State Parks as well from all over the region.

Besides myself, I had brought Cheetah, another game warden, to assist, borrowed from his patrol boat assignment at Moss Landing along the coastline. I had trained Cheetah when I was teaching at the California Fish and Game Law Enforcement Academy, and once out of training we started to work together on a regular basis. We became friends quickly, and besides running marathons and training for firearms competitions together, we were always getting involved in good cases between the coastline and the inland foothills of my district.

Cheetah was fast, levelheaded, good with a rifle, and in great overall physical shape for hiking and eradicating operations anywhere. For his first eradication mission, he was pumped.

The plan was simple. Two teams would converge on the grow site during the takedown. I would lead one team in from the top of the canyon just like GI and I had done several weeks before. The second team, made up of California State Park Rangers and two officers from the Santa Clara County Sheriff's Office, would hike upstream from the bottom of the canyon. Stationing themselves just below the last garden site, these officers would be in position to catch any growers who got away from the team above if they fled. During the briefing, introductions were made and allied agency bonds began to form as the teams met and coordinated with each other. When the briefing concluded, we all went home to prepare our equipment and get to bed early for the pre-sunrise detail just a few hours away.

After a 4:00 a.m. meeting of all team members and convoying up to the stone ranch house on the Palassou, we gathered our gear and weapons. I took my team of twelve officers to the top of the ridge. Once in place, we set up positions on the ridgeline above the creek giving the second team time to make its hike to the bottom edge of the grow site to set up and wait for my team to move into position.

Mike, the State Park Ranger overseeing the second of our two teams, took his group into the dry creek bed and started the long upstream hike with his people. Mike's team had a longer hike in distance and time than my team did. His team had to move exceptionally slowly over the rocks in the creek bottom to avoid being heard by the growers above.

After a forty-five-minute wait, with Cheetah right behind me, I slowly moved the team down the ridgeline toward the creek bottom. My goal was to bring us into the creek at the exact location where GI and I had entered previously. This would give us a starting point hidden from any growers below us while also ensuring a quiet approach route into the garden.

We moved in ranger file formation with each operator 3 or 4 yards from one another and rifles on ready. We moved in this way to avoid injury to the team as a whole in the event we were ambushed. No one spoke; instead we used hand signals and head movements to communicate with each other. Quietly moving a team that large into an area so remote, wooded, and steep was difficult. It was especially tough to keep the team completely quiet as we descended the ridge toward the creek bottom. Dry grass, rocks, and loose dirt made slipping down the steep hill and making some noise impossible to avoid.

Reaching the edge of the creek, I froze for a few seconds before scanning the area slowly and carefully with my rifle. Nothing moved around me, and it appeared our group had made it down the ridge without detection. Still early in the morning, visibility was poor and the light minimal. I stopped my scan and looked back at Cheetah to ascertain the status of the rest of the team now spread out above us. As if reading my mind, Cheetah nodded and took a head count in the dark woods. He looked back at me and patted his head and nodded, giving the signal that everyone was accounted for. I nodded and held my left hand in the air before waving it forward directing the rest of the team to move toward us. Like trees coming to life on the dark hillside, ten camouflaged men packing assault rifles emerged from the woods and began to move slowly downhill. It was an ominous sight, and it was clear we meant business that day.

Once together, and because they were the lead enforcement team for this operation, the UNET members took over on point. Cheetah and I rotated a few positions back in the stack of operators and once position changes were made, we moved down the creek, slowly following the waterway to the first grow site.

As we hiked downstream in the creek, I could see two men sitting next to the tent in the kitchen area of the camp. We could smell hot food cooking on their camp stove, and it was clear they were preparing their morning breakfast. About 50 yards ahead of our team's position, these two growers talked quietly and listened to music softly playing on a small portable radio. The entire team stopped moving, and the two task force officers at the head of the pack kneeled down behind some logs in the creek bottom to watch the pair ahead.

The task force's main objective of the day was to eradicate plants and to apprehend growers if possible. Chasing cultivation suspects was discouraged. If a chase occurred, however, no less than two officers could pursue a suspect, a wise decision for officer safety reasons.

From their position up front and covering the two men with their AR15 rifles, task force operators Dave and Jaimie called out, "Police! Don't move, and put your hands up!" The two growers jumped up and instantly started running downstream in the creek bed. They were too far to pursue, and being away from the front of the stack anyway to start a chase, I looked at Cheetah and we both sighed with frustration. Chasing them would be pointless given their head start, knowledge of the area, and planned escape routes. At least they were headed in the direction of Mike's blocking team below and hopefully would be picked up.

Even though the men were gone, Cheetah and I elected to follow their trail until we reached Mike's team. The rest of our team would verify the garden areas were empty of any growers and start eradicating the crop once the area was declared safe. Cheetah and I jogged down the creek bed, scanning and passing marijuana gardens on the banks above both sides of the creek. We had been running for almost 600 yards and had been passing gardens all along the way. When we reached the bottom of the final grow site, I stopped and announced by radio we were coming downstream to Mike's team. Not wishing to surprise the team below and be mistaken for a grower on the run we waited to hear back. Within seconds, Mike told us the area was clear and to come on through.

When we reached the lower team, Mike told us both growers had almost run right into them. Before reaching the team, however, the men made a fast left turn and ran straight uphill and into the brush above the grow site. Mike got a good look at the two growers, describing one as in his late thirties and stocky, while the other was younger, very thin and fast, and in his early twenties. On the ground in front of Cheetah was one of the men's sneakers. The pair had turned and run so quickly uphill one of them had run right out of his shoes!

It seemed to me these men should have been caught given our team's positions that morning during the assault. As I pondered this, Snake appeared with his partner, Paulina. They were assigned to the MET of the Santa Clara County Sheriff's Office, and I had met both of them just briefly during the operations briefing the day before. I later learned Snake was an accomplished martial arts instructor, big-game hunter, and a veteran police officer with experience in field training officer and tactical team instruction.

Dressed in the distinct tiger-striped camouflage BDUs worn by the sheriff's office SWAT team, which is called the Sheriff's Emergency Response Team (SERT), and carrying a nicely camouflaged AR15 carbine with a Trijicon advanced combat optical gun sight attached, Snake looked serious. The "sniper" tab above his subdued department shoulder patches signified he was a precision marksman and part of a small and elite team in SERT. The olive-colored sweat cloth wrapped around his forehead gave Snake the appearance of a military Special Forces operator, and the calm and determined look in his eyes behind his small rimmed glasses conveyed seriousness. I knew instantly I liked this guy.

As he approached, Snake looked at me and said, "Trailblazer, I'm not comfortable letting these guys just run away while we stand around. We've got nothing better to do at the moment so what do you say we do some tracking?"

"Good idea, Snake. Cheetah and I are with you," I replied.

With that, we turned uphill and started following the broken brush trail the two growers had left behind when fleeing frantically up the hill. They were long gone, but for the next hour Snake, Paulina, Cheetah, and I tracked them as far as we could. The men were clearly hiding out in Dexter Canyon over the hill, and finding them would be next to impossible if they just stayed still and hid throughout the day. At least we had tried to do something. At the time I didn't know that working with Snake that morning would lead to many more operations together in the immediate future. We liked each other's mind-set, how we worked together, and we quickly developed a friendship as well. Even more compelling were the near-death experiences we would share on operations with the rest of our team members in the years to come.

After abandoning the tracking attempt, all four of us returned to the grow site and began eradicating and counting plants. By the end of the morning, the teams had destroyed 7,500 plants spanning a half mile of creek bed. Once pulled from the ground, all of the plants were placed in large stacks before being airlifted out. Once lifted above and out of the garden site, the plants were placed in the large cargo beds of trucks where they were then delivered to a dump site and burned.

With most of the team too exhausted to hike out of the canyon at the end of the day, Eric, the UNET team leader, pulled out a satellite phone and called for air support. After a brief phone conversation with the Team Hawk pilot from the 129th Air Rescue Wing of the California Air National Guard out of Moffett Field, Eric had good news (Team Hawk is the statewide narcotics enforcement designated call sign for the helicopter team). We were all getting hoisted out by helicopter. No more hiking for the team that day.

When we were told about the helicopter extraction, I had no idea what type of bird Eric was referring to. Thirty minutes later, when the deafening roar of blades chopping the air above us signified the helicopter's arrival, I was quickly educated. The Pave Hawk helicopter, used for military search and rescue operations all over the world, was impressive. When hovering several hundred feet above us, the 100 mph rotor wash was so powerful it bent large-diameter trees to the ground as if they were willow branches. Just to stand up underneath the bird without being blown over took a lot of effort. Ironically enough, as the rotor wash bent all the tree branches near the landing zone to the ground, I could see a fresh three-point trophy-size blacktail buck antler set nailed to one of the trees. We later learned one of the growers had poached and killed the majestic animal just days before our raid, nailing it to a tree as a trophy display. It was clear that the men running this grow operation had no respect for the wildlife and the natural resources that surrounded it.

As the Pave Hawk hovered above our landing zone, one of its PJs (an Air Force Special Forces pararescueman who is tasked with recovery and medical treatment of personnel in humanitarian and combat environments) was lowered by hoist to our position on the ground. The PJ had two helmets and two rescue harnesses for us to use. After a quick training session on how to use the harness and hoist, the entire team would be extracted in pairs from the ground into the chopper several hundred feet above us.

The Pave Hawk pilot was unfamiliar with the area and needed to find a good landing spot for the bird. Given my familiarity with the ranch topography, I was asked to go up first and assist the pilot. I looked over at Cheetah and waved him over to the landing zone next to the PJ. We placed the harnesses under our arms as instructed and stowed our packs and rifles behind us before being lifted off the ground. Neither of us had done anything like this before, and with the deafening roar of the Pave Hawk above us and the ground getting farther and farther away below us, the excitement and adrenaline rush was overwhelming. After what seemed like forever, we were being dragged into the side of the Pave Hawk by another PJ and were given safety belts for the duration of the ride. I directed the pilot to put the bird down near an old barn just south of the stone ranch house.

For the next two hours, the team worked with the Pave Hawk crew to get all the marijuana out of the woods, onto trucks, and disposed of off site. Thinking again about the environmental destruction in that remote canyon, I knew I would follow up on this site to conduct a cleanup detail well after this day's eradication operation was complete. Reclaiming and restoring the creek channel to get the water quality back on track would be a good starting point, but it would take time for the creek to heal.

At the end of the fourteen-hour day, Cheetah and I said our good-byes to all the team members before heading home. On the way to my truck, Snake approached us, and with a smile on his face asked me for a business card saying we needed to stay in touch. He also asked if I liked the idea of working together again on one of his operations in the future. Cheetah and I looked at each other and smiled before I told him to name the place and time. Snake grinned back at us and said he would call me. We all laughed as we turned to part and start the drive off the Palassou Ridge and back home after a long, exciting, and productive day. I could already tell it was going to be a very interesting summer.

CHAPTER 2

Gunfight on Sierra Azul: One Man Down

Enemy occupied territory—that is what this world is.

—C. S. LEWIS

Large pools of blood were forming on Mojo's pants around both wounds and had started to drip onto the ground. This was not a good sign. Blood loss and shock were now Mojo's biggest threats. Mojo was too young, too dedicated, and too deserving of a full career as a game warden to die on this remote hill on his first eradication operation.

When we started this mission just a few hours ago, seeing Mojo in this condition was the last thought that crossed my mind, and something that our newly developing team had not ever come close to experiencing before. Today was a wake up call to the seriousness of what we do and a reminder of the war we fight every time we gear up and hike into the bush for an arrest and eradication mission. This is the story of the day the MET's preparation and approach to all future operations changed forever.

❖

The day of August 5, 2005 started in a church parking lot on Hicks Road on the outskirts of Los Gatos just shy of 6:00 a.m. As I rolled up in my green pickup, my partners from the Santa Clara County

Sheriff's Office MET were already there, drinking coffee and swapping stories at the back of their Jeep. It was good to see Snake and his buddies, Rails and Apache, dressed in tactical gear and the trademark tiger-striped camouflage of their unit.

I had not worked with Apache yet but had heard good things about him. Apache was a marine and was involved in extensive combat in Beirut, Lebanon, in the mid-1980s when our embassy needed protecting. And I also learned that morning that Apache, like Snake and Rails, was one of four snipers for the sheriff's office, which is known throughout the profession as an exceptional sniper team.

When seeing him for the first time, I was impressed. His lean and medium-height frame translated to fitness and agility in the woods. And the deliberate look in his eyes as we talked was comforting. Without even discussing our personal experiences yet, I suspected he had known conflict in the past. Whether it was in a law enforcement or military role I did not know, but he had definitely survived some dramatic engagements. Apache looked ready for anything we might encounter. His camouflage was set up perfectly and all his tactical gear subdued in color to blend perfectly with the surrounding woods. I could tell from the elaborate camo job on his AR15 and optical sight system that he meant business.

Right after shaking hands during introductions, he looked at my short-barreled M14 and asked, "Hey, Trailblazer, is that a military M14 or an M1A scout? The barrel looks too short to be an M14 but that flash hider is straight M14. What's the deal?" Impressed that Apache knew his firearms I replied, "This is a Springfield M14, Apache, built sometime in the late 1950s. Military spec through and through with a shortened barrel and the full auto selector switch removed and pinned for semi-auto-only capability."

After learning that this was a Department of Fish and Game issued patrol rifle, Apache's face lit up. "Damn, Snake, I like these

Fish and Game guys! Any agency that carries a rifle like that is good to go in my book!"

That morning was also the first time Rails was involved in an eradication operation since joining the team earlier that spring. Cheetah and I had met Rails for the first time at the Campaign Against Marijuana Planting (CAMP) two-day short-haul training school at Camp San Luis on California's central coastline just a few months before.

CAMP is a Department of Justice task force that utilizes five or more helicopters and associated ground teams throughout the summer marijuana harvest months throughout California. CAMP helicopters drop ground teams into garden sites to eradicate marijuana gardens and destroy the cash crop in a particular region of California.

While our MET enjoys working with CAMP very effectively on missions throughout the season, our teams have different enforcement objectives and styles. CAMP teams primarily drop into and get out of garden sites by helicopter, eradicating and removing plants along the way. Except in extreme cases where hiking access is excessively difficult, our MET teams hike into each garden to arrest any growers working their crop before we begin eradicating plants at each site. When we're lucky enough to have CAMP's assistance on missions, we're able to short haul out of grow sites and back to the command post at the end of the mission. When possible, this avoids an arduous hike at the end of a tiring day of hiking and eradicating plants in hot summer temperatures.

Attending the class alone, Rails introduced himself to Cheetah and me at the training session, and the three of us instantly bonded and hung out for the duration of the class.

The newest and youngest member of MET, Rails' constant smile was infectious, and it was hard not to like him instantly. In this business Rails' humble, humorous, and outgoing personality was refreshing, and he has always been a consummate professional and a pleasure to work with. Also a SERT sniper, Rails was the youngest and newest precision rifleman on the sniper team and also Snake's only full time partner and newest member of the MET. Skilled in map reading, GPS coordination, fugitive tracking, backcountry operations, and radio communications, Rails' skills were invaluable to the team. And over the years his navigation has led the team into some nearly impossible to find grow operations.

The green pickup parked next to the Jeep belonged to another warden, code-named Bulldog, who was on loan from the San Mateo/Santa Cruz County Fish and Game warden squad. That day was Bulldog's first major tactical operation on this side of the hill. As Bulldog was gearing up in his tactical vest, I noticed a large machete hanging from his belt. I couldn't help but grin upon seeing the over-sized knife, a sign of Bulldog's eagerness to take down a dope grow.

Minutes later, my Santa Clara County partner, Mojo, arrived with Ben, a ranger for the Midpeninsula Regional Open Space District. Mojo, as always, was pumped. He had been working the area for only two years, and, like Bulldog, this was his first big grow operation.

Ben was our guide that day and he knew the trail like the back of his hand. He was instrumental in finding this particular grow last year on the Sierra Azul property managed by his Open Space district. The ridge where we would be working was part of the park, but was off-limits to the public because of its inaccessibility and ruggedness. Ben had already guided Snake into the area for reconnaissance. It would later become apparent that he could hold his own when the crap hit the fan.

This day was the first operation of the new season. Our goals were to eradicate the lucrative crop, arrest any growers or guards residing in the grow, assess and rectify any environmental damage created by this illegal practice, and above all stay safe.

Just a couple of years ago, few members of the public were aware of the Department of Fish and Game's involvement in marijuana eradication operations—and were even more unaware of why we were involved. The grow operation we found in 2004 in a remote canyon on the Palassou Ridge property summed up the reasons. Seven thousand five hundred plants were spread out over a half mile of creek channel, a creek that had supported red-legged and yellow-legged frogs, steelhead trout, and other sensitive aquatic species. We found the grove by observing that the channel was stone dead. Many miles up this rugged canyon, the growers had dammed up the creek in several places. Large quantities of fertilizer, pesticides, and other pollutants were found in the pools created by the dams, and were dumped directly into the watercourse for the purpose of supporting the crop, regardless of the cost of destroying the creek's wildlife resources.

In addition, all bank vegetation and tree life along the edge of the channel had been destroyed to clear areas for marijuana plants. This in turn created a major siltation and erosion issue for this channel once the winter season began just a few months following harvest time. Making matters worse, we found several mammal carcasses and a trophy three-point antler set of a blacktail buck taken by the growers for food. Once I witnessed how much these marijuana plantations negatively affected our wildlife resources, I committed myself to eliminating this problem to the best of my ability. My fellow law enforcement colleagues shared my sentiments.

After camouflaging and gearing up, Snake conducted his briefing. Today's mission was solely a MET operation without the help of SERT or other assistance. Our team was comprised of operators from the sheriff's office and the Department of Fish and Game and our team was small. Overall, the plan was simple. Our team of seven would covertly hike up a ridge off Wagner Road and quietly infiltrate the plantation. The ridge ahead of us was steep and brushy, with lots of manzanita, oak trees, and coyote brush to conceal our approach to the garden.

Ben would guide us to the edge of the grow and then move to the back of the pack and wait as we continued on to clear the area. Clearing the grow entailed detecting and removing any booby traps if present. The primary clearing objective, however, was to find, arrest, and handle any growers in the plantation, as well as secure possible weapons. Only after these objectives were met could we begin to eradicate the crop.

Snake and Rails had arranged for the Region 3 CAMP team to assist us in eradicating the grow once it was secure. Once our team secured the scene on the ground, CAMP would send team members in via helicopter. During short haul operations, two men are hooked in to a long line under the helicopter, standing upright, and then the helicopter slowly rises until the men on the wire are lifted up. The helicopter gains a little altitude, with the two men hanging below, before they are carried through the air at a speed of 70 to 100 mph, a few hundred feet over wooded terrain up to a distance of 5 miles. When reaching the target area, the two men are lowered into a landing zone. This gets a team in quickly, and also avoids the men's having to wade through the poison oak that growers seem to like to surround their groves with for protection. After the plants have been cut down, the helicopter carries them out in large bundles, and then comes back for the men on the ground.

The briefing was short. Within minutes, we were convoying in our patrol trucks to the end of Wagner Road. Once parked, we gathered, conducted a final equipment check, and loaded our rifles. Before moving out, and with the sun beginning to rise behind us, I took a final look at Mojo and Bulldog and gave them the thumbs-up. They returned the sign with the fire of excitement in their eyes. Feeling the same rush, I joined the rest of the team, and we began hiking up the ridge.

Even with cool temperatures, hiking any type of steep grade on uneven terrain with tactical gear, long guns, and ballistic vests is a workout. That day was no exception. The temperature was already over eighty degrees at that early morning hour as we pushed up the steep ridge. Sweat began to pour. Everyone maintained his distance from the others, careful not to push too close or too far. Mojo and Bulldog followed behind me, with Snake, Apache, Rails, and Ben ahead of us.

As we came within 50 yards of the first grow site, Ben stopped on the trail, and one by one we moved slowly past him. Word was passed down the line that we were getting close, which meant we would have to belly-crawl along the trail under a very low canopy of brush. I saw Snake drop to a crawl ahead of me. One by one we began crawling through the brush and ground cover holding our rifles in front of and across our bodies in an effort to remain quiet. With my nose so close to the ground, the seasonally strong, earthy smell of brush reminded me that the beginning of deer season was just a week away.

The low crawl trail ended on the edge of the first garden where the marijuana plants began in a tight and confined area of brush cover. It wasn't until we entered the garden that we could stand up straight.

The first plants were over 6 feet tall. Because the crop was so thick, we were concerned about booby traps—a bear trap, a pitfall, a trip wire attached to a gun, or worse yet, a grower hidden in the garden. Snake flashed a hand signal to me that we would be moving in two teams of three. The first team (Apache, Rails, and Bulldog) would work slowly through the garden to the southwest, while the second team (Snake, myself, and Mojo) would work to the northwest.

The teams were now staggered throughout the garden in one long skirmish line, moving slowly and silently in the same direction. With situational awareness at its highest and noise discipline maintained, everyone moved at the same slow pace to keep our coordinated distances and detect any booby traps. If one or more of us ended up too far ahead of the rest of the team and a firefight erupted, we could potentially end up in a deadly crossfire situation.

As our movement progressed past the first grow and into a second larger garden, we could see that this was a very sophisticated operation. I could not believe how big and healthy most of the plants were. Some were over my head, well above six feet. Each plant had an individual drip watering line feeding it from a larger central water hose. The water pipe (the common half-inch black plastic variety) was elaborately camouflaged with forest green spray paint. Next to one of the water lines was a five-gallon bucket, half full of a dark blue liquid I suspected was a pesticide and fertilizer mix of some kind. Like the water line, the bucket was also carefully camouflaged in forest-green paint. The attention to detail was impressive. It was obvious the growers involved were not amateurs.

As we moved through the second garden, I noticed that the area was simply too quiet and the garden was too still. Birds did not chirp, and although we should have heard animals moving through the brush around us, we heard nothing. It was so quiet in fact, that all I could hear was my slow breathing, and all I could see moving was Snake's slow and deliberate stalk through the grow just a few yards to my right.

Ahead of my position, I could see the end of the crop. The garden ended at the edge of a large brush pile (apparently the remnants of brush removed by the growers to clear an area for their plants) that completely blocked the view up the ridge ahead of us. When I reached the edge of the garden, I stopped inside the concealment of the plants and just waited. I was now in the front of the pack, with Apache and Rails to my left and Snake to my right. Mojo was a few yards behind me, and Bulldog was not far behind him.

Perhaps it was because of my years of hunting experience or just dumb luck, but I sensed the need to stop and observe. Something was not right. Maybe we were being watched. Was the brush pile a barrier to what lay ahead? I maintained my position on the edge of the garden while holding my M14 rifle at the high ready position and scanned slowly ahead left to right.

Several of the team members later remembered hearing voices—Spanish words spoken quietly ahead of our position near the brush pile. The voices were faint yet stood out on the unusually quiet ridgeline. What the men were discussing we will never know, but I suspect it had to do with us.

Within seconds of hearing the voices in the brush, a single rifle shot cracked the silence. The shot was close, very close, and my mind immediately identified the weapon as a medium-bore rifle, most likely a 7.62 x 39 Russian, the caliber of the Soviet AK47 assault rifle. My heart skipped a beat immediately. I was certain of one thing: no one on our team possessed a weapon of that caliber, and the shot must have come from the growers. (Fish and Game officers carry the M1A M14 .308 caliber rifle, which is much louder than the shot we heard. Our colleagues from the sheriff's office on the other hand were all carrying the M4 carbine, a .223 caliber weapon our military uses around the world. The .223 is a small rifle caliber and has a distinctly different sound from the shot we heard.)

Immediately following the shot, Mojo yelled, "I've been hit, the bastard shot me! I'm shot!" Right after hearing this, I heard numerous rifle shots from Snake and Apache's M4 carbines several yards to my right. Realizing my partners were now in a firefight with a grower ahead of us, I swept my rifle toward that direction in an effort to provide cover. Because the garden was so dense, I could not see what Snake and Apache were shooting at. Moments later, however, I learned that one of the growers had stood up in the brush pile ahead, pointing a shotgun directly at us. Fortunately for us all, Snake and Apache shot and dropped the grower before he had a chance to return fire.

As I moved toward Snake to provide support, I noticed movement in my peripheral vision, slightly left of my position. As I scanned back toward the movement with my rifle, I saw a second grower. The man was dressed in drab green-colored military clothing and wore a green military-style cap. More importantly, the grower held a rifle with both hands at the port arms position, carrying the rifle across his body with the barrel pointed to his side. The grower was walking around the brush pile toward Mojo, Bulldog, and me. This man had fired the single shot that hit Mojo and was now apparently coming back at us to finish the job. As he approached, I raised my rifle toward the gunman and started to identify myself. As soon as I started my announcement, the man saw me and pointed his rifle in my direction while simultaneously dropping down and out of view into the brush. As soon as his rifle pointed toward me, I retreated toward Mojo and fired at the grower as I moved. I fired three times in rapid succession, and ended up in a kneeling position next to Mojo's right leg when the shooting ended.

I have been told by other law enforcement officers that everything is quieter than expected during a firefight. This was true here. All the gunfire, including the shots I fired from my loud M14, sounded muffled to me. So muffled that it sounded as if I were wearing hearing protection. Time also seemed to slow down. The gunfight appeared to take forever, and all of Apache's and Snake's carbine shots seemed to be spread out over a long period of time before I fired my rifle. In reality, however, the entire firefight (from the first shot that hit Mojo until the completion of the final shots fired by all three of us) lasted only a few seconds.

After the shooting had stopped, I swept the area through my rifle sights and no longer saw the gunman. I paused, took a breath, and just listened. The woods were quiet once again. I did not know if the grower I shot at was hit, but at this point it didn't matter. Both gunmen had been stopped from continuing their attack on our team. Now, securing Mojo's safety and tending to his wounds was our priority.

Snake alerted the rest of the group that he had a suspect down who was probably dead in the brush pile which we would not be able to confirm until many hours later. I responded that I had engaged another armed grower who had disappeared behind the brush pile. Snake called out to team members to check their status. Everyone answered with the good news that no one else was hit. I called out to the team verbally and told them that Mojo had been hit and that we needed to establish a perimeter around him. Hearing this, Snake quickly retreated to our location. He positioned himself left of me, placing Mojo between the two of us. Rails retreated and positioned himself to Snake's left side. Without saying a word, Apache also retreated and positioned himself just ahead of us to my right. Still on my rifle and scanning down range, I called out to Bulldog. In his typically calm and collected fashion, Bulldog quickly yelled out that he was all right and that he had already set up behind us to cover our backs.

Ben, the last member of our team, stayed on the eastern edge of the garden when we started our sweep through the area. When the shooting started, Ben was positioned behind us all. Ben had been told by his bosses to be a guide only and not enter or help secure the garden with our team. Following the gunfight, Ben dropped to a low-profile, prone position to watch our left flank to the southwest, completing a solid perimeter. For an unarmed ranger, this took real guts.

An operation like today's was not within a typical day's work for Ben. However, given his motivation and concern for criminal activity occurring in the more remote areas of his agency's property, Ben took the extra effort and steps to investigate this grow site and help with its destruction. Unlike game wardens who work large areas of wooded terrain environments spanning several jurisdictions, park rangers typically work one specific park area within their agency's property boundaries. Also unlike game wardens, who focus on environmental and wildlife crimes in their particular districts, park rangers are more generalized in their mandates, and handle all aspects of law enforcement and public safety issues. And unfortunately like most ranger staff from smaller local agencies, Ben was limited in doing comprehensive law enforcement functions safely due to a lack of adequate protection equipment. Since Ben's agency does not allow or train their ranger staff to carry firearms and other force option tools to handle aggravated enforcement contacts, Ben's law enforcement capabilities are limited.

With the 360-degree perimeter established, I talked to Mojo and tried to assess his wounds. It was obvious he was seriously hurt. But he was also strong spirited, as well as pissed off. Mojo said he had been shot through both of his legs. He thought the bullet had entered the left leg and exited before passing completely through his right leg. After being hit, Mojo dropped to the ground. Unable to effectively handle his rifle, Mojo placed his M1A on the ground and drew his pistol. He was applying pressure to stop the heavy bleeding on the inner thigh area of his right leg with his left hand while holding his Glock 22 duty pistol in his right hand as we talked. He was by no means out of the fight, but was losing blood rapidly.

As I tended to Mojo, Rails conveyed our situation to his dispatch by radio and requested everything from medical air support to tactical team operators needed to secure the hill. I monitored Mojo and called our dispatch. Unbelievably, my cell phone had service, and I was able to reach CENCOM (Central Communications Center for the Department of Parks and Recreation in Monterey, California) and tell Captain Huck, my immediate supervisor, and Sarah what happened. For the remainder of the operation, our crisis was coordinated through the sheriff's dispatch center.

We stretched Mojo out for his comfort and elevated his legs when I heard Apache telling Bulldog to hand something to me. Seconds later, Bulldog handed me two military gauze bandages with green webbing ties attached. Guided by Mojo on the necessary pressure and tension of the dressings, I covered and tied off both leg wounds within a few minutes. The bleeding in Mojo's legs began to slow significantly.

We were told a medical helicopter had been dispatched and was fifteen minutes away and that a California Department of Forestry (CDF) Huey helicopter was also on the way equipped with a medic and stokes basket or litter, which is a type of stretcher with a backboard used to extract the injured. The medic and basket were necessary to take Mojo safely off the hill and transport him to the medical helicopter that would be waiting at the landing zone. From there, that chopper would fly him directly to Valley Medical Center in San José. The CDF chopper had an arrival time of fifteen minutes as well, or so we were told. We were also advised that a team of paramedics was on its way from where we started our hike and would be coming up the hill on foot behind us to assist. Their arrival time was projected to be forty-five minutes. If only any of these times had been close to accurate.

Watching Mojo stay positive and fight through the pain of his wounds during this long wait was both agonizing and inspiring. Watching him suffer was awful, but the strength and fighting spirit he maintained throughout the whole incident was an inspiration to us all. In addition, we all knew that less than 30 yards ahead of us was the potential danger of the gunmen, whose locations were still unknown.

After his wounds were dressed, Mojo looked up at me and said, "Trailblazer, I'm doing fine. It hurts, but I'm going to be fine. Next week we have a deer opener to handle. I'm going to work a full career as a game warden and retire from this job! I'm going to retire as a game warden!" I told Mojo that he needed to keep fighting because I had big plans for future operations together. Mojo smiled and replied that he knew we would be working together again in the future, and that he would be back in the woods busting wildlife poachers after his recovery.

Immediately following this conversation, we heard movement in the woods ahead from the area where the gunman had disappeared. The sound of someone crawling through brush ahead of us was distinct. It appeared that one of the aggressors we had engaged was slowly moving around ahead of us. Snake acknowledged hearing this as well. Snake and I continued to scan ahead intently over our rifle sights through the dense marijuana crop surrounding us. Snake suddenly yelled, "This is the sheriff's office! If you're still out there you better run because if you show up again you will be shot! You better run now because we will find you!" The anger in Snake's voice meant business. The movement in the brush ahead of us lasted only a few more minutes before the woods were quiet again.

Moments later, I heard Bulldog behind me move and retrieve his cell phone from his vest before whispering, "Hello?" . . . "No baby, I'm okay. It wasn't me. Mojo was shot but he is okay. We all are.

How did you know? . . . Great. Well, don't listen to any press reports because they're wrong. Mojo was shot, not anyone else. Okay. I'm still on the hill and it's dangerous so I have to go. I'll call you as soon as I can." With that, Bulldog finished the call and looked up at me before saying, "I don't know how the press got wind of this so fast, but Sierra just saw our story on the morning news and it's all over the networks."

The firefight hadn't been over for fifteen minutes and already the media was broadcasting a story that had not been confirmed. Sierra, Bulldog's fiancée, had learned of our incident and was panicked. While the rest of the team maintained perimeter security, one by one each of us took a turn on our cell phones to call our families and let them know our status. Fortunately, Mojo was able to reach his fiancée, Callie.

Shortly following the phone calls, a CDF helicopter flew slowly across the ridgeline. The helicopter, a UH-1D Vietnam-era Huey, was the perfect chopper for the operation. Equipped with a medic, winch and cable, and a stokes basket, it could drop a medic and a basket quickly into a landing zone within our perimeter. Mojo could then be airlifted off the hill and flown directly to the hospital for surgery. This solution seemed simple and efficient. Upon seeing the Huey, we thought Mojo was just minutes away from leaving the hill, but then the helicopter crew advised Rails they could not see us because of the thick cover and our camouflage, and asked us to signal the chopper. No one in our group had a signal mirror. Fortunately, Apache handed Bulldog a smoke flare from his pack, and Bulldog took the flare and ignited it. A large dense plume of orange smoke rose above our position in the tall garden. The helicopter crew acknowledged seeing the smoke cloud and marked our location for rescue.

Then the helicopter immediately turned around and flew out of the area back toward Los Gatos. We were shocked. Why were they leaving us? The crew had our location pinpointed, and we could see the medic hanging over the open bay door with the basket and cable in his hands as the chopper circled above us. But instead of dropping the medic with the basket and retrieving Mojo, the helicopter flew away. Rails checked with his dispatch center over the radio to find out why the chopper left. Seconds later, Rails told us that the helicopter crew was directed to stay out of the area until the hillside was secure from possible sniper fire from the still unknown location of the growers. Until operational commanders within the sheriff's office deemed the area secure, the chopper was directed to stay away. Snake, Rails, and I tried to mask our frustration the best we could, but we were shocked.

In an attempt to get answers without alarming or panicking Mojo, I turned my head toward Rails and asked quietly, "Why the delay, Rails? Why are they leaving?"

Rails replied, "It's not right Trailblazer. They told me a minute ago they would be here in 15 minutes, and now they are telling me they can't come in at all until the area is completely secure!"

I was enraged and snapped back, "That can't happen! We need them here *now*. Mojo's going to bleed out and he is already exhausted from fighting shock this long!"

"I know," Rails responded. "There is no way we can completely secure this area even if we had a larger team. This ridgeline is way too big and densely wooded. It's going to take all day to secure. I'll keep pushing them to get us help pronto!"

Shaking my head in frustration, I told him, "Let's hope for it sooner than later. I don't know how much longer Mojo can hang on."

When I turned my head back toward Mojo, he looked up at me and asked where the chopper was going. As I explained the situation to him, Mojo was shattered and the look of frustration and defeat on his face was heartbreaking. Obviously in excruciating pain, Mojo just shook his head and told me this was bullshit. He was right. Someone needed to take a chance and help us or we were going to have a dead young warden on our hands.

For the next two hours we waited and maintained our perimeter. I continued to monitor Mojo for vital signs, and we talked every few minutes to make sure he was conscious and coherent. His legs were elevated, his head rested on my daypack, and my CamelBak hydration system was placed within easy reach for him to sip water. Mojo continued to maintain high spirits and even threw out several jokes when the long periods of quiet silence became uncomfortable. After about two hours into the incident, and many more status update requests to the sheriff's office dispatch center, we were still being told the helicopter would be there soon. Like the rest of us, Mojo's confidence in our air support was deteriorating rapidly. We were all frustrated with the delay, and while the rest of the team guarded our perimeter, all I could do was tend to Mojo, and impatiently wait for help to arrive. I felt compelled to do something and could wait no longer, so I called the sheriff's office dispatch center and identified myself. I advised the dispatcher it was my warden who was shot and told her we had waited far too long for help to arrive. When she heard this, the dispatcher was shocked and told us she thought we had paramedic support already with us on the ground. I told her that was false. Within a few minutes of that conversation, Rails was advised that the helicopter would be returning to our location to start Mojo's extraction.

Knowing that help for Mojo was finally coming was a huge relief. In thirteen years as a game warden, this was the most difficult event I had ever faced in the field and certainly the most dangerous any of us had faced at work. Having been a squad supervisor for only two months prior made the event that much more challenging and difficult to work through. I was used to taking care of myself and operating independently with little supervision as a game warden in dangerous situations, but it was much more challenging to ensure the safety of my squad members, especially in situations as violent and uncontrollable as today's gunfight.

Waiting for help to arrive, and knowing I had little control over the outcome of the day was agonizing and something I was not used to. Today was testing the mettle of Snake and myself as team leaders, and putting us face to face with the possible death of not only a team member, but for me a partner who was at the start of an outstanding career. Keeping Mojo as calm and comfortable as possible while also stifling my frustration and helping keep the team calm was all I could do now. Used to being in control and making things happen, I had to adjust my thinking and realize there was only so much any of us, me included, could do in this situation. Along with the rest of the team, I needed to wait and realize that much of today's outcome was in God's hands and that we were all doing what we could for Mojo.

Before a helicopter could lower a basket and medic to us, we needed to clear a landing zone. Between the tall marijuana plants and other heavy brush cover, the chopper had no place to safely deliver equipment and personnel. Bulldog calmly volunteered. "Hey, Boss, I'll cut a landing zone behind you and Mojo with my machete. I can see a good area right behind you guys that shouldn't take long." Bulldog would have to break cover by standing up to cut away the vegetation. It would be risky, but he understood and would get it done. Snake and I raised ourselves up to a high kneeling position with our rifles, providing better cover for Bulldog while sacrificing some cover ourselves.

After a few minutes of hacking and chopping, Bulldog had cut a perfect 8-foot-by-8-foot-square landing zone. After completing his project, Bulldog sat back down next to me and continued to guard the rear perimeter. Once Snake and I dropped back down into position, I promised Bulldog that I would never give him crap again about packing such an oversized machete into a garden.

The waiting game resumed. Fifteen more minutes passed. After a long silence from the entire team, Mojo called out to me and said, "Hey, Trailblazer, I feel different. I don't know if I'm just tired or what, but I want to go to sleep." I told Mojo, "Stay awake, just fight to stay awake," and I kept talking to prevent him from slipping into unconsciousness. My heart began to race and I was terrified. I thought this was it. As tough as he was, Mojo was fading. There was nothing more we could do for him, and my patience was gone. I looked at Rails and asked him to inform dispatch that Mojo had just gone into shock, was unconscious, and that we were losing him. Rails made the call.

Within minutes we heard the chopper returning. The helicopter crew informed us again that we were still not visible. We had no more smoke flares and were without a signal mirror. While the team brainstormed a solution Bulldog remembered the operational plan he had folded in the pocket of his cargo pants. The plan was printed on several 8 1/2 x 11 sheets of white paper, and the back of each page was blank and bright white. As I refocused on the sights of my rifle and scanned ahead, Bulldog stood up and flashed the sheets toward the chopper. Rails announced that the crew had spotted the signal paper and had located us.

As the chopper hovered above our perimeter, we heard the paramedics coming up the hill behind us. Just before they reached us, Mojo looked up at me, grabbed my arm, and pleaded, "Whatever happens, Trailblazer, don't let them take my legs! Don't let them take my legs, okay?" I told Mojo I would do everything I could to prevent it. The thought of my partner losing his legs to this battle in the infancy of his career was frightening, and it simply could not happen.

Just as the medics arrived behind us, the helicopter lowered its altitude and hovered less than 100 feet above our position. The rotor of the Huey caused so much wind on the ground that what was a shadowy forest of heavy brush and marijuana plants just seconds before was transformed instantly into a defoliated and flattened ridgetop without any cover or concealment. We were suddenly sitting ducks, easy targets for any gunman wanting to take another shot at the team. The chopper's rotor was loud, and the booming concussion of the big helicopter's blades cutting through the air was deafening. If a shot was fired at us now, hearing it and locating its point of origin would be difficult. The wind and noise coming from above was fierce, and the sudden brightness of the penetrating sunlight overwhelming. As I continued to scan over my rifle sights, I jerked my head back and forth repeatedly as large marijuana plants were blown around my face, slapping me from all directions.

Wearing blue coveralls and carrying small medical trauma bags, the two medics who walked into the area looked tired, sweaty, and overwhelmed. This was obviously not a normal service call. Without taking my eyes off my rifle sights, I described Mojo's wounds and told them Snake and I would cover them as they worked on Mojo. I added as diplomatically as I could that they needed to be quick about it.

They wasted no time. One medic cut away Mojo's BDU pants at the knee line to assess the bullet wounds. I took just a few seconds to look at the damage to Mojo's legs. I was shocked. Mojo's left leg, where the projectile had first entered and then exited, was bloody with moderate-size bullet holes on both sides of his leg. The wound to his right leg, however, was unreal. Because the bullet was tumbling when it exited his left leg, it entered in a keyhole fashion and tumbled aggressively before passing through and exiting. Like any well-designed military battle cartridge, the 7.62 mm projectile did exactly what it was designed to do, and unfortunately it tore his right leg apart. A softball-size chunk of his inner thigh, from the center of his leg out to the skin, was missing. All that remained was a large, bloody cavity where muscle, skin, and fatty tissue once had been.

How Mojo did not bleed out and die from these wounds I will never know. How we were able to stop the bleeding and control the shock his body was fighting for almost two and a half hours is a mystery. The medic informed me that no bones or arteries appeared to be hit, and regardless of the tissue damage to both legs, Mojo would keep both of them. I reiterated to the medic how important it was for Mojo to keep his legs. The medic smiled and said, "Don't worry, Lieutenant; I think he's going to be okay. I was slightly relieved but not entirely convinced. We still had to get Mojo safely off this unsecured hill and to the hospital.

The Huey moved in and hovered directly above us. As Mojo was being bandaged, stabilized, and given an IV for hydration, the chopper crew lowered a basket and another medic. Once on the ground, the medics moved Mojo on to a backboard basket to prepare him for a short-haul ride to the incident command center. The medic warned Mojo that moving him was going to be painful. On a count of three Mojo was lifted off the ground onto the backboard. Even over the deafening roar of the Huey above we could hear Mojo's painful scream. The adrenaline was wearing off, and the pain was excruciating. Seconds later, Mojo, with the helicopter medic at his side, was lifted off the ground and into the air and evacuated. The chopper with Mojo hanging underneath became smaller and smaller until he was finally out of view and flying toward the landing zone.

Suddenly we heard more footsteps approaching from behind us, and we went on high alert. We breathed a sigh of relief when several sheriff's deputies carrying long guns appeared. Just coming off all-night-patrol assignments and wearing torn and dirty uniforms after a hike through thick brush, these officers stepped into our perimeter. One by one, more support officers arrived to relieve us. As more help arrived, Snake, Apache, Bulldog, Ben, and I maintained our positions and continued to scan ahead for potential threats. Until adequate perimeter relief was completely in place, we would not leave.

I glanced over to Snake and asked, "You know what we need before we leave this hill?"

Snake replied, "What's that?"

I answered, "Ten more minutes, just ten more minutes to advance to the brush pile and see what we've got."

Snake agreed and said, "I'm all for that. We can move forward and start tracking if necessary." Snake then called out ahead of us into the brush, "What do you think, Apache?"

Apache's eagerness was obvious in his response, "Yeah, I'm ready to move when you guys are!"

Unfortunately for us, the incident command staff had already made the decision for us to stand down. Because the three of us had been involved in the shooting and had been on the hill for so long, we were not allowed to advance past our perimeter. Command staff members figured we were fatigued and stressed enough for one day. Given the morning's events, commanders did not want us hunting down armed and violent growers anymore that day. Instead, SERT team members were assigned to do that job, and we were to be extracted from the hill for immediate debriefing.

Within seconds of the Huey's departure, the CAMP helicopter moved into position above our landing zone. The crew had been flying perimeter sweeps above us throughout the morning, and those guys were chomping at the bit to drop some operators into our perimeter to lend some help.

The Jet Ranger helicopter moved toward our location, and I could see two CAMP operators suspended below the chopper on a short-haul cable. These officers helped insert SERT operators into the shooting site and extract us from the hill.

Once the CAMP operators landed inside our perimeter, one of their officers asked who needed to be extracted from the hill first. Hiking back down the ridge would take time none of us could afford. A high-speed ride underneath the CAMP chopper would be ten times faster. Because it was my squad member who was shot, I requested that Bulldog and I leave immediately so we could check on him at the hospital as soon as possible. Fortunately, I had attended short-haul training and certification just two months before. Bulldog, however, was entering uncharted territory.

We quickly strapped into short-haul rigs, the four-point rescue harnesses cinched down on our bodies as we hustled to prepare for the imminent helicopter ride. Because Mojo had been extracted without any of his tactical gear, we had to transport it with us. Between the two of us, we had to carry Mojo's M1A rifle, his Glock 22 pistol and belt system, his tactical vest loaded to capacity with gear, all in addition to our own gear. Bulldog slung Mojo's rifle over his tactical vest and placed Mojo's pistol belt over his arm. I put Mojo's tactical vest over my backpack. Bulldog and I looked a lot like a camouflaged version of the Michelin tire man.

I looked across at Bulldog and told him to lock his legs in mine as we lifted off the ground. I then told him that we would be moving fast through the air once the chopper cleared the brush canopy, and that he would have to help me keep us from spinning once we were moving cross-country. With one hand on the suspension line under the helicopter and my other hand out to my side, I gave the signal for the chopper to lift, and we were quickly off the ground. As we rose above the brush canopy, I took one last look at the perimeter team below and then looked directly across at Bulldog. Less than 2 feet in front of me was Bulldog's face, eager and a little overwhelmed. While still climbing up above the hillside I heard Bulldog say, "Hey, Boss, did I ever tell you I'm scared of heights?"

"I hope you're joking," I replied, "but if you're not, whatever you do, do not look down at the ground and do not look up at the chopper. Just look me in the eyes and talk to me as we fly." Bulldog nodded his head.

Rising above the canopy of marijuana and heavy brush, the Sierra Azul mountain range became much smaller until we were several hundred feet above the treetops. As we reached a peak altitude, the CAMP pilot turned the chopper northeast and increased the bird's speed. When short-hauling people, CAMP helicopter pilots generally travel between 70 and 100 mph. As we increased speed, I knew our air speed was closer to the high end of that range. And as our air speed increased, the wind pressure on our faces and noise in our ears increased as well. To prevent us from spinning uncontrollably under the helicopter, I extended my left arm from the side of my body while holding the harness line above us with my right hand. People being moved in this way can also use this technique to pivot up to 360 degrees in any direction under the chopper if they need to turn to see a particular area below.

As we flew east toward the incident command center, Bulldog looked me directly in the eye and yelled over the wind noise, "You know I may never do this again. I've got to look around and see what's happening around us even if it makes me sick!" I told Bulldog to go ahead but to close his eyes quickly if he started to lose it. I watched as Bulldog nodded his head downward. As soon as his eyes looked away and down from mine I heard Bulldog let out a prolonged yell, "Whooooaaahhh . . . we're going fast!" Within seconds he was looking back at me with eyes as big as silver dollars.

People who are unfamiliar with the types of operations I'm involved in often ask me what it is like to short-haul under a helicopter. Is it scary? Is it exciting? Do you feel vulnerable and exposed under the helicopter during a flight? Do you worry about the pilot making a mistake or the helicopter crashing? Do you worry about being face planted into a tree? The answer to all these questions is yes. Short-hauling is very exciting and you absolutely do feel exposed under the chopper when ripping through the air at 100 plus mph suspended only by a thin steel cable. Overall, you need to have a lot of confidence in the pilot, and our confidence in the CAMP pilots has never wavered. Regardless of the danger involved, short-hauling is exhilarating, and like a hawk catching a thermal draft to soar across the treetops at maximum speed, short-hauling is the closest you can get to flying without having wings yourself.

As we continued to fly toward the incident command center, I looked toward the rapidly approaching town of Los Gatos below us. In the powerful wind of flight, a sound swelled up from my guts and I yelled. I yelled for Mojo, yelled because the operation turned deadly, yelled for the rest of the team, and yelled for the toll this event would take on all of us. Mojo was just starting his career, and for all I knew it could be over before it really got started. And finally, I yelled out of shear rage. I wanted to lay waste to that hillside and hoped that every armed grower running through those woods was gone, wiped out before more damage could be done. I later realized that yelling as loud as you can while flying 100 mph suspended 300 hundred feet above the ground under a helicopter is incredibly therapeutic.

Within minutes, we could see the incident command landing zone quickly getting bigger. Numerous people from all levels of the operation assigned to specific tasks were on the large grass field. Several fellow law enforcement officers, both uniform patrol and special operations personnel, were on the ground preparing for the next phase of securing the grow site. Press cameras and reporter crews were present. Bulldog and I decided that as soon as we touched down, we needed to get away from the cameras, find someone from our departments, and get to our vehicles to secure our gear. Seconds later, I gave the pilot the hand signal to touch down and release us on the ground.

Now here comes the part you never see on TV. After stowing our gear and returning to the incident command center, we were directed to the sheriff's office headquarters for debriefing and interviews related to the incident.

Before reaching the sheriff's office, I was told that the Department of Fish and Game's Shooting Investigation Team was on its way from Sacramento to assist in the investigation. Racing from her job at the district attorney's office, my wife, Char, was also on her way.

The investigation process at the sheriff's office took the entire afternoon. Having never been a participant in an officer-involved shooting before, I was apprehensive. Since I was one of three shooters involved in the gunfight, I would be interviewed last, as would Snake and Apache. Nonshooter witnesses like Bulldog, Rails, and Ben, would be interviewed first.

For the next four hours, all of us involved in the gunfight waited our turn to give statements for the investigation. I waited for my attorney to arrive to brief me before the interview began. Mark had the reputation of being one of the top attorneys to represent officers involved in shootings.

Because a blood sample was needed to check for the presence of drugs or alcohol, I was not allowed to eat anything until a technician arrived to draw my blood. Since the last food I had eaten was during the briefing at 6:00 a.m., I was ravenous. Watching all our partners eat sandwiches and sip cold drinks was tough as we waited. When the technician finally arrived and finished taking our blood samples, sandwiches and drinks tasted like the nectar of the gods.

All I wanted to do was finish the interview and get to the hospital to check on Mojo. Before starting the questioning, Chief Bravo (who was heading up the shooting investigation team for my department) informed me I had the option of selecting one enforcement officer from my department to sit through the interview process in addition to my attorney. I could think of no one better than my longtime friend and mentor, Bravo himself. Bravo's experience in this area was not isolated to his law enforcement role. His combat experience in the military, most notably in the jungles of Vietnam, gave him an understanding of what my team had experienced. Bravo and I had become respected colleagues and friends over the past thirteen years of my career.

The small room was equipped with a table and chairs to seat two homicide detectives from the sheriff's office, an investigator from the district attorney's office, my attorney, Bravo, and me. The interview was taped by a video camera and two audio recorders. The interview was efficient, formal, and professional, with the reason why I had fired my rifle at a suspect being a key question. While obvious to those of us on the team in the gunfight, I paused a minute before answering. With all the drama and excitement of the day to this point, I had not thought about the ramifications of using my rifle in today's gunfight.

Like Snake and Apache, I had done what I train others to do and was trained to do myself to protect me and my fellow officers from death or severe injury. I realized then that my hope of getting through my entire law enforcement career without having to use any of my issued firearms on another person was over. I wanted to be clear that my decision to press the trigger of my M14 to stop the attacking grower was necessary and within the deadly force policy of my department. Following my answer there were no other follow up questions regarding my decision to use deadly force. I think the violent attack on our team and the aggressive nature of the morning's ambush said it all.

After the interview, Bravo and I had a minute to talk alone. As we walked, Bravo stopped me, put his hand on my shoulder and said, "You did a great job up there today. You did everything you were trained to do and led your guys well. Whatever you do, do not second-guess anything about how you handled yourself today. Like all shootings, and I would know, you will relive today's events over and over. You will have dreams about the shootout and think of everything else you could have done differently. Don't. You did it right today, and I'm proud of you." As Bravo shook my hand I thanked him for his support. With that, we left the hallway and walked back into the briefing room. Inside I saw Bulldog who had waited several hours for me to finish my interview. He was determined to stay with me so we could go to the hospital together. The Shooting Investigation Team, Bulldog, and I left the sheriff's office to caravan to the hospital.

At the hospital formalities were dropped as we exchanged hugs of support and heard words of encouragement from our Chief of Patrol Nancy Foley and the Director Ryan Brodderick. Carmela, the Assistant Chief of my district, led me around a corner in the hallway and told me that Mojo had just come out of surgery and that the doctor had not yet passed on any information regarding his condition. After hearing this from Carmela, Bulldog and I walked to Mojo's room to meet Callie, Mojo's fiancée, and his parents. They looked shaken but positive. I assured them that Mojo had done a great job on the hill and that he stayed strong and professional throughout the battle.

The doctors also thought he would recover completely and come back to work in several months. The wave of relief I felt was huge.

Bulldog and I entered Mojo's room by ourselves. While he looked disoriented from surgery and the pain medication, Mojo had a look in his eyes that was comforting. Right away, he was leaning up from his bed, eagerly wanting to talk about what had happened. Bulldog and I wanted to talk about the shooting just as much as Mojo did, but we knew that until all formal interviews were completed, we could not. This was frustrating but necessary. I just hoped Mojo would be interviewed soon so we could start talking about the event. Doing this would be critical for us to work through the cauldron of feelings stirred up by the shooting.

Instead of discussing the shooting, the three of us talked about how different the day had turned out from what we had expected. I asked Mojo, "Hey buddy, how you feeling after all this craziness today?"

Mojo replied, "I'm tired but I hear the surgery went well and that I'm going to recover. I'll make it back to work after I heal." Still groggy and heavily sedated from the surgery, Mojo was fading in and out. "I saw so much ahead of us in the garden today before I got shot and hope we can talk about it soon."

Shaking my head in agreement I replied, "I know bud. We have a lot to talk about and getting you plenty of rest and recovery time first and foremost is the key now. Just remember you did an amazing job today fighting through the shock and waiting that long after the shooting. And you trying to protect yourself and the team even after you were shot was amazing. I'm so proud of you Mojo, and if I can do anything for you during recovery and beyond, just reach out okay?"

We continued to talk and given the circumstances, laughed a lot and were grateful to be alive and together. As we talked, Mojo started to fade in and out of sleep again, and we knew this was our sign to leave. Mojo had family who needed to be with him during the night; and we both had our families we needed now as well. Bulldog had not seen his fiancée, Sierra, the whole day. With that, we said good-bye. We knew that over the next several days we would be back to visit with Mojo.

Finally, Char and I were the only ones left in the parking lot. She just looked at me and smiled before saying, "Crazy day, sweetie, and I love you and I'm proud of you. Let's go home now." I looked at the setting sun above us and was amazed at how much had happened in the past thirteen hours. As Char drove away ahead of me, I hesitated for a minute before climbing into the seat of my patrol truck and turned toward the setting sun. Still dressed in dirty and sweaty camouflage BDUs from the morning's operation, I was elated to be alive, angry that we had been ambushed, and saddened that Mojo had been hurt. But even as chills ran down my back, I felt blessed.

After numerous doctors' appointments, physical therapy sessions, and long days of exercising his legs a little at a time, Mojo healed and recovered throughout the fall and toward the end of 2005. He came back to a full-duty work assignment in January of 2006, and while he continues to attend physical therapy several times a week and suffer from sore muscles following a strenuous day of hiking, the shooting has not slowed him down in the least. Mojo continues to do good work, take on exceptional cases, and, most importantly, remain positive toward recovering 100 percent. His attitude is truly inspiring to all of us. His return to duty was nothing less than extraordinary. In 2007 Mojo received the prestigious Pogue-Elm Award from the Western Association of Fish and Wildlife Agencies and was named the Department of Fish and Game's Warden of the Year, the highest performance honor a game warden can receive in this profession.

The investigation revealed that the man Snake and Apache killed was not the man who shot Mojo. That gunman was armed with a 12-gauge pump action shotgun in his hands and a .22 caliber pistol on his belt. When Snake spotted him, the gunman had the shotgun pointed toward me and Mojo with a live round of buckshot in the chamber and four more rounds in the magazine. The man who shot Mojo was the gunman I saw and engaged. This man was armed with some variant of a 7.62 x 39 caliber Russian rifle, as the one empty casing found at the crime scene verified. His actions were deliberate. I am certain this gunman intended to finish the job he started when he moved around the brush pile with his rifle trained on Mojo and Bulldog.

To this day, this shooter has not been found. Informants through the narcotics network allegedly placed him in the central valley a few days following the shooting, injured from a bullet wound. This man has apparently been identified as a Mexican national with several felony warrants for various violent crimes. I'd like to think the bullet wound rumor is true and that his wound has kept him from committing more violence wherever he is. One can only hope.

Following the shooting, all of us involved in the gunfight were placed on administrative leave. Under their department's policy,

Snake and Apache were off for two weeks following the shooting. I, on the other hand, was directed by my department to take at least five days off to recover, with more time off available if needed. More than anything I did not want to stop my momentum. I hated the idea of thugs halting our progress. My colleagues at the sheriff's office, now in the peak season of marijuana suppression, also could not afford the down time. Regardless, we all took the mandatory breaks for our benefit and prepared mentally and logistically to return to the field.

Once the tension of the weekend subsided, I found the time off to be welcome. And, like any driven game warden who has just received a brand new patrol vehicle after six years, I spent many hours meticulously working on my new truck, prepping it for field operations. All of these things helped pass the time and kept me busy, but I really needed to get back into the woods with my colleagues.

The whole experience of marijuana eradication operations was different now, with the stakes higher and the growers having no qualms about shooting law enforcement officers. The level of violence and firepower we had encountered, combined with the remoteness of all the gardens we were finding, upped the ante on the danger related to this kind of work. My anxiety grew when I thought about going back to eradicate another dope grow, but I knew we had to do it. Only by getting back in the woods and raiding more grow sites could we feel vindicated.

The bond shared by men who survive and work through a gunfight is amazing. When the violence starts and the bullets fly, it doesn't matter why you are there. What matters are the guys next to you, relying on you to keep it together and cover them just as they would for you. And these bonds strengthen and continue to grow through more time in the field from operation to operation.

Within a week of returning to work, Warden Bones (my only

other squad member and Mojo's partner warden), and I participated in a total of four eradication details within a single week in
San Benito, Santa Clara, and Stanislaus Counties. Now that the
word was out that Fish and Game had a stake in these operations
and its staff had survived a gunfight during a detail, we were getting
requests for help from all over the state, especially locally. While
the operations that week progressed smoothly, with some arrests
safely made and thousands of plants eradicated, it was just great
to be back on those details. It was even better to be working with
Snake, Apache, and Rails, our teammates from the sheriff's office.

Two weeks after the shooting when our teams were back
together for eradication details in south Santa Clara County, Apache
and Snake were excited to tell me they had received approval to
purchase four .308 caliber, 16-inch, short-barreled Springfield
M1A SOCOM (Special Operations Command) rifles. These rifles
would be used for rural SERT and MET eradication details where
increased shooting distances and barrier penetration were necessary. The significantly better performance and barrier penetration
capabilities of the heavy .308 caliber bullet in a wooded and brush-
laden environment were appropriately determined to be essential
for these operations. Because so many of the .223 caliber bullets
fired by Snake and Apache had deflected in the heavy brush before
reaching their target, the MET team decided to push toward a
change for the better. Now with their operators using the SOCOMs,
both of our teams carry the same rifle system and have magazine
and ammunition compatibility.

In January 2006 Mojo, Bulldog, and I hiked back up to the shooting
site for the first time since the incident. As we moved carefully up the

ridgeline and through the area of the gunfight, we could see crime scene tape and flags identifying critical evidence from the shootout. The presence of these items appeared surreal and out of place in a now serene and peaceful stretch of woods. With the exception of these investigation markers and the barren ground left by the removal of the abundant marijuana plants, the ridgeline was unchanged; a snap-shot in time taken six months earlier and revisited now that many months later. For the first time, we hiked past the shootout site and into other large grow areas and a camp. The camp was large and obviously used by many growers operating on several other ridge-lines to the north and south of our location. The magnitude of how large this grow operation was in years past quickly became evident. The camp looked like it could have been used that day. Cooking gear, camouflaged tents, clothing, food stashes, animal traps, buckets of animal parts, and various other items of camping comfort remained scattered around the main camp. Again, it appeared as if the camp's occupants had simply vanished without a trace and without leaving so much as a footprint.

Repercussions from the shooting continued to pass through our lives. Almost six months following the incident, Mojo, Snake, Apache, and I testified before the Santa Clara County grand jury on January 24, 2006, regarding the shooting and its justification. Unique to Santa Clara County, any officer involved in a shooting, regardless of how justified and legally appropriate, must go through a grand jury that reviews the circumstances of the shooting and determines the legal and moral justification of the officers when deciding to use deadly force. If such force is deemed appropriate, the officers involved are cleared by the grand jury and no further review is needed. If the grand jury concludes that deadly force was used inappropriately, however, an indictment can be handed down, and the officers involved can be prosecuted for various levels of murder. Having never testified in front of a panel like this before, all of us were a little apprehensive about the process. Regardless of the confidence in our actions on the hill, the stakes were high and the level of judicial review intimidating.

The unique part of a grand jury is its large size and duration of service. The panel consists of twenty-three people who deliberate for a specified period of time on several cases. A jury foreman, as opposed to a judge, sits on the judge's bench and facilitates the review process. With the exception of the district attorney, no other attorneys are present for the defense or to represent the officers involved. This is quite different from a conventional twelve-member criminal jury that reviews one particular case and cannot ask direct questions of anyone testifying in the court proceedings.

Starky, the special prosecutor appointed by the attorney general and brought in from another county to present the case, was great to work with and prepared us well for the event. Starky made sure we had a good idea of what to expect. One by one, each of us were called in to answer the district attorney's questions, explain the order of events, describe the terrain and shooting scene, and answer any questions individual jury members asked. The grand jury members had few questions for me, and their support for our actions on the hill that day was evident.

For the next five days the team waited anxiously to hear the grand jury's findings. On the following Monday, Snake called me with the news and faxed me a copy of the jury's decision. In the third paragraph of a succinctly written four-paragraph letter addressed to the sheriff, Starky concluded:

During my investigation, I visited the scene of the shooting, viewed all of the physical evidence, interviewed the officers

involved in the shooting and reviewed the investigation con-
ducted by the Santa Clara County Sheriff's homicide inves-
tigators. I concluded that all of the officers . . . fired their
weapons in self-defense and in defense of others and were
legally justified in shooting and killing. . . . At the conclusion
of my investigation, I presented my findings to a Santa Clara
County criminal grand jury. Those proceedings concluded
yesterday with the grand jury deciding not to indict any of
the officers involved.

While we had little doubt about the outcome of the grand jury process, because anything can happen during a trial, these words were a huge relief and gave a sense of closure to the incident as a whole. With the trial now behind us and the Department's support for arrest and eradication operations continuing, Mojo, Bulldog, and I received the California Department of Fish and Game's Medal of Valor in 2006. For his injuries, Mojo also received the department's Purple Heart, while Bulldog and I received the department's Lifesaving Award for our actions on Sierra Azul on August 5, 2005.

Following our department's support, the next year on December 4, 2007, Bulldog and I were presented Medals of Valor by California Governor Arnold Schwarzenegger for "extraordinary acts of bravery and heroism" during the August 5, 2005, shootout on Sierra Azul Ridge.

When Mojo was shot, I heard alarming questions from a variety of public entities and other law enforcement agencies. Questions like "Why was Fish and Game there?" and "Isn't that a job for the police?" especially agitated me.

While these questions were asked mostly from ignorance, Mojo's shooting actually gave Fish and Game some well-deserved and drastically needed attention. The fact that we are highly trained and professional officers was finally becoming known. Very few law enforcement officers are comfortable, or knowledgeable, when operating in remote and rugged terrain in such small groups. Fish and Game wardens, however, operate in this environment on a daily basis, and see it as second nature. We are at home in the woods. When I started my career, I knew it would be dangerous working in the woods. What I never fathomed, however, was that our forests could be so violent with the addition of so many illegal cultivation operations occurring on our public lands.

Our firearms and tactical training is equal to that of some of the most progressive local, state, and federal law enforcement agencies throughout the country. I am proud to be one of several trainers responsible for maintaining this high level among our troops throughout the state. My sheriff's office colleagues embraced me before this detail based on our past operations together. Mojo and Bulldog, however, were new to this type of work so early in their careers and were new faces to our allied agency partners that morning when we met for the briefing. Immediately, Snake made it clear in his briefing that both new wardens were accepted as part of the team based on a reputation and work ethic game wardens have exhibited throughout Santa Clara County.

Bulldog and Mojo showed their professionalism during the crisis. Their level of tactical training and teamwork mentality helped keep all of us alive that day. In addition, Fish and Game was privileged to have Snake, Apache, and Rails at our side; they are three of the most skilled and motivated sheriff's deputies I have been privileged to work with.

Did we do anything wrong tactically on the hill that morning as some have speculated? The answer to that question is a resounding *no*. Everyone involved, as either trainers or operators, dissected our tactics that morning. We all agree that with the exception of using more people and additional teams to flush the growers into a waiting arrest team (which was not possible that day), we would not have changed our tactics that day. Like any mission of this type, there is no way of knowing what we face each time we go on a mission. Without the additional personnel, that luxury was not available that day. Because of the shooting, we would get more staff support in the future and as a result have more tactical options when executing these operations. It is a shame we had to experience a gunfight for this to happen, but it is a great improvement. Mojo was shot because the growers knew their environment well, had great concealment, and were prepared to shoot anyone in order to protect their garden. Given their preparation and advantages, it amazes me that more officers were not shot or injured. It is even more impressive that the two gunmen only shot once during the whole firefight because of the rapid response of our team as a whole.

CHAPTER 3

Montebello Foot Pursuit: Light Runners and a Patrol Dog Come to the Rescue

The dog has been esteemed and loved by all people on earth. He has deserved this affection because he renders services that have made him man's best friend.

—ALFRED BARBOU

It was a warm mid-May afternoon in 2008. Things were kicking into high gear for another year. Besides normal patrol duties, I was averaging two scouting missions each week with the MET.

Snake had called me earlier in the week about some fresh intelligence regarding possible cultivation activity in north Santa Clara County. Over the past few weeks homeowners living on Montebello Road, located in the foothills west of the quiet community of Cupertino, had reported seeing strange men in camouflage walking along the road during early morning and late evening hours. These men were observed descending into a steep canyon east of Montebello Road that was alarmingly close to some custom homes in the area. Like with so many other grow operations in this area, the public property in question was owned by the Mid-Penninsula Regional Open Space Authority.

At first glance one would not suspect organized criminal cultivation activity could happen in such a quiet, affluent, and very low-crime area, but looks can be deceiving. Because of year-round water sources and steep, brushy, and difficult-to-access canyons getting plenty of summertime sunlight, the Montebello Road area is actually a prime spot to grow marijuana. We had come to learn that from past experience.

This day's plan was different from past scout missions. Since the shootout on Sierra Azul, our team considered scouting missions to be as dangerous and high risk as arrest and eradication operations. Given this, we agreed to scout throughout the season in groups of at least two operators armed with long rifles. Ideally, though, we agreed to have four of us on a scouting mission when possible. This way, if the team did encounter growers attempting to stalk in or out of the grow site or had the opportunity to eradicate a grow safely and efficiently early in the season, the team could deal with the situation that day. We all agreed that not having to come back a second time later in the season when MET and Fish and Game operations were in a constant frenzy was preferable.

The team on this day consisted of Snake, Apache, me, and a four-legged asset, my patrol dog Jordan, a nine-year-old female yellow Labrador retriever and a Department of Fish and Game companion dog since 2005. She has been instrumental in finding poached deer, fish, firearms, and marijuana gardens during her tenure as a department K-9, and she is great for public relations as well. Snake, Apache, and all the other members of MET have taken a liking to Jordan over the past years and now consider her part of the team.

The plan was simple. Snake, Apache, Jordan, and I would stalk slowly and silently downhill on a well-worn foot trail Snake had found. There were signs that it was being used, so we were certain this was the growers' main access to their grow site deep in the canyon below us. Our goal was to locate a grow site and any growers in the garden without being detected. We wanted to avoid contacting anyone in the grow that day if possible. We needed to know the layout of the garden, the camp, and where to expect growers when we came back with a large arrest and eradication team later in the season. Our goal was not only to eradicate the grove but to catch as many of the growers as possible later during the planned arrest and eradication mission. Past experience has shown that the biggest population of growers gathers around harvest time, which typically starts in August.

As we descended on the trail into the canyon I had no doubt that we would find an active grow site. The trail was too well worn to mean anything else. With Snake on point, and Apache, me, and Jordan following, the team moved forward slowly, constantly scanning ahead. As we reached a level spot on the trail, Jordan stopped and froze, the hackles on her back went up. She then raised and bent her front left leg, her pointing signal for an animal or a person ahead.

Just as Jordan signaled, Snake held up his left hand and made a fist, signaling everyone behind him to stop and freeze. He too had apparently seen something ahead. Slowly Snake kneeled down while scanning through his Aimpoint, the electronic optical sight on his AR15 rifle. Apache and I followed suit, both of us kneeling down and off to the side of the trail behind Snake. Familiar with stalking and stopping silently on numerous hunts in the past with me, Jordan also kneeled down.

Once concealed on the trail, Snake leaned back to us and whispered, "Two growers and plants, 50 yards out. Looks like both of them are next to a garden and a kitchen area and have tools in their hands." Apache and I nodded as I slowly pulled out my pocket binoculars. As I glassed the brush ahead, I could make out the two men, walking back and forth past some supplies stacked against a hillside in the brush. Canned goods in various colors and cooking supplies were on the ground around them. Both men were dressed in dark earth-tone colors, indicative of the camouflage these organized groups use to blend in with the terrain and avoid detection.

I glassed carefully for guns on both men. It was hard to tell with them moving around so much and all the brush in the way, but we had to try. As the Sierra Azul shootout proved, these men were more often than not armed and would fight if confronted. And in our experience, grow sites in the northwest Santa Cruz mountain area of the county seemed to have more guns and more men willing to use them than other garden sites throughout the region. Maybe this was just a coincidence, but we were not taking any chances.

For the next forty-five minutes we watched the men moving and working throughout the garden site before they moved out of view north and away from our position. We had seen all we needed to for that day. Now it was time to get out of the area without being detected and do some planning. Since Jordan and I were in the back of the stack, we were first to move. In a reverse bounding overwatch, or leap frog as it is sometimes referred to, the team started to retreat out of the grow site. I whispered "Moving," and without taking their eyes off the threat area, Apache and Snake responded, "Covering," before Jordan and I slowly stood up and backed out of the area on the foot trail. Once stationary and out of view of the growers, and with Jordan leashed next to me, I provided long cover with my M14 as Apache and Snake moved back past our position. Taking turns we did this for about 50 yards before hiking the remaining distance on the trail and out of the grow.

Once we were back at our vehicles, I loaded Jordan in my patrol truck before we took a minute to debrief the day and go over our next move. All three of us agreed this grow site had a great trail going into it and warranted using a quiet, experienced team complete with light runners, operators carrying handguns and very little gear, to stalk and catch suspects come raid day. We also realized that because of the terrain challenges and the steep hill almost 700 feet below the road leading to the grow and a future command post, this operation needed helicopter support and the CAMP team. Also, given the size of the plants we had viewed, we knew this grow had to be eradicated as soon as possible before the bandits had a chance to harvest. This would be the first eradication on our agenda for the season. Instead of making it to illegal sale for profit, these plants would be destroyed, removed from the grow site, and buried in a deep landfill before that could happen.

Less than two months later, our team assembled before sunrise on July 9 at the top of Montebello Road. This was the first of a two-day operation with our primary MET team members and the assistance of the Region 3 CAMP team.

Like previous MET operations, the plan was simple. Two arrest and security teams would go down into the canyon to clear the grow and locate and arrest suspects if possible. Once the grow site was cleared of all threats and all trails in and around the garden were assessed, the CAMP teams would be short-hauled in by helicopter to eradicate and remove the high-dollar crop.

For the two-day operation the team was fortunate to have Warden Cheetah and his partner, Markos, in town to help out. On loan from another district in northern California, both were skilled in these and other backcountry operations and could be trusted by everyone on the team to handle anything heavy we might encounter.

My Santa Clara County partner for the first five years of his career, Markos and I had seen a lot of action together. A skilled backcountry operator, Markos had completed SWAT, handgun, carbine, submachine gun, and sniper rifle schools with me. Markos is one of the most competent and levelheaded shooters I have had the pleasure of working with and is 100 percent trustworthy.

During those five years, we teamed up to work numerous back-country surveillance poaching details. Deer baiting and hunter trespass cases that often took several weeks to complete were our norm in the deer hunting season. These cases usually occurred in the middle of summer with temperatures reaching into the 100s and required long, uncomfortable hours of stalking into and out of an area undetected—just like the skills needed for effective marijuana arrest and eradication operations.

In addition, these crimes usually happened in locations as far away as 20 miles on a dirt road necessitating the use of four-wheel-drive patrol trucks, all-terrain vehicles, and long foot hikes. Following that up with even longer hours of surveillance, often overnight, in a wooded surveillance hide made our arrests that much more satisfying for both of us. Busting a poacher in the remotest area of the backcountry where he or she may have been committing wildlife crimes year after year without getting caught is the most rewarding job a game warden can do. These are the types of cases Markos and I gravitated toward as much as possible, and, consequently, a strong bond developed between us. No matter how long the day was or how rundown we became, Markos never backed down from our objective. I had come to trust Markos and Cheetah and my other MET brothers with my life in any situation.

Also in the mix for the day's operation were Spag, Doc, and Woody. Spag is a firearms training sergeant for the sheriff's office and a part-time member of our MET. As the leader of his department's sniper team, Spag is one of the most organized and meticulous snipers I have ever known, and like the rest of the MET team members, he is solid on his firearms, field craft, camouflage, and stalking skills. Soft spoken in general, Spag's seriousness is apparent regardless of what he is doing. Markos and I met Spag for the first time when we were all students attending our first sniper school almost a decade ago. Sponsored by his department, Spag was a deputy training to be on the sniper team, and the three of us had the opportunity to shoot and train together all week. Given his attention to detail and helpful nature I liked him immediately. I had no idea at the time we would be working so closely and intensely together ten years later, but I enjoy every minute when we do.

Whether teaching a sniper school, running range training for in-service officers and special operations team members, or stalking bandits in a marijuana garden, Spag's willingness to help and support a fellow operator on the team stands out. Spag will literally give the shirt off his back to a team member if needed. That operator will, however, get the typical Spag critical question of "What the f--!" for all of us to hear when it happens, but Spag has a genuine heart.

Doc is also another part-time member of the MET. A reserve sheriff's deputy and paramedic, Doc is an invaluable member of the team. Since we did not have him to help during Mojo's shooting in 2005, Doc has been added to our team, and we have him on as many eradication operations as possible now. Doc is also a skilled trauma medic always equipped with a large field backpack full of trauma medical supplies. These supplies are all handpicked to keep us alive in case of serious injuries such as gunshot wounds, broken bones, deep cuts, heat stroke, dehydration, and such.

Woody is another asset to the team and very nontypical when it comes to team supervisors. Serving as sergeant in the MET throughout the entire 2008 eradication season, Woody's level head and calm approach to problem solving in a crisis event was well suited for our team, and his intimate knowledge of the team's mission was an asset. While overseeing the team, Woody supported and was involved with his operators on every level of eradication operations. This included being part of the arrest and eradication team and going *into* the grow sites with us. Woody is the only supervisor in the history of the MET to go in with the team on operations, thus giving him a hands-on understanding of the varied issues we face during such details. The next two days were going to be the most dangerous and challenging forty-eight hours our team would face to date, and having Woody there on behalf of the sheriff's department was a comfort.

For the morning's operation we were fielding two teams. The point team was a chase and arrest team, while the second team was a quick reaction force (QRF) behind the point team. The point team, which was the lead team, consisted of six men with Snake and Spag up front. Right behind them were Cheetah and me as light runners, with Markos and Rails behind us for additional support.

The secondary team, the QRF, run by Woody, also had six members including Doc. Never more than about 50 yards away from the point team, the QRF was just a radio whisper away for support if things turned critical up front. If we encountered resistance on our stalk and needed help, the QRF would move up quickly and fill around behind us providing cover.

Just before sunrise, with the trail below Montebello Road just visible enough for the team to navigate, the point team descended a dirt chute onto the well-worn trail. Each one of us moved silently down the trail until everyone on the point team was together. We stopped for a minute to let the dust settle and listen for any movement. What greeted us was an eerie silence, with not even a bird, squirrel, or other animal sound around us. On the ground were fresh human tracks, tennis shoe footprints going downhill into the grow site. So fresh, in fact, these two men were only a few hours ahead of us and had apparently hiked the trail in complete darkness to avoid detection. The trail was well worn, and brush and other leaf litter were beaten down into the dirt. It looked like a public park hiking trail that was getting daily foot traffic. This indicated one thing—an early harvest time—and we all hoped we had not missed the prime processing and harvesting operations for this garden. The next few hours would tell.

With Snake and Spag creeping slowly downhill on the trail, Cheetah and I followed silently behind them. I could not hear Markos and Rails behind me, but I knew they were there.

For the next forty-five minutes our point team moved slowly down the trail before Spag held up his right hand in a closed fist directing the team to stop. We were not yet at the kitchen area where we had seen the growers a few months previously, and I was curious what Spag saw up ahead. Whispering into his radio, Spag told us he had movement 50 yards ahead. Slowly all six of us kneeled down on the ground before freezing and assessing the threat up ahead. With my mini binoculars I could see what Spag was seeing through his rifle optic. Three men, directly across a small canyon ahead of us to the east, were processing marijuana in a cluster of small manzanita trees. All three growers were unaware of our team's presence as we watched them while they continued to work away. We now had the advantage. Our team could set up for the light runners, Cheetah and me, to stalk closer and shorten the distance to the growers for an inevitable pursuit on foot.

As runners, Cheetah and I knew we needed to get as close as possible to be effective and catch these guys. We all knew what was next having discussed this plan well ahead of time. After past seasons of trying to chase and then losing several suspects, I thought a change in tactics was in order. All of us on the MET were just too weighed down and limited in our agility with long guns and tactical gear to effectively chase and catch anyone we spotted, even if we did get close to the person.

Before this season started, I discussed the light runner concept with Snake and Rails. Both thought it was a good idea to try, provided we could find at least two fast and agile runners for each grow operation. To be done safely, the runner teams would have to be safely covered by skilled long gun operators up front. This would allow the runners, armed only with handguns and light arrest equipment, to move safely toward growers. In today's operation, Cheetah and I had Snake and Spag, two of the best long gunners and situationally aware operators covering us.

Snake and Spag each positioned themselves behind a large log just below the trail we were on. Balancing their rifles on the log, both operators were scanning and covering all three men with their rifle optics as Cheetah and I prepared to stalk closer to the growers. Both of us peeled off our backpacks and left them on the trail behind us. Armed now with only our handguns, handcuffs, pepper spray, and minimal arrest equipment, we were set to move toward the suspects. Cheetah and I were equipped so lightly for one reason only: to be as fast and agile as possible and have the best chance of catching a grower during pursuit.

One rule of being a light runner is to never chase anyone alone. Even if pursuing a single suspect, runners always chase as a team. In fact a MET rule is that no one follows a trail, suspect, or checks a grow site without a partner and radio communication.

Effective runners have to be in good physical condition to run quickly and be capable of covering long distances; they must be able to navigate quickly and maintain their balance across uneven, rocky, and heavily wooded terrain; and they have to be able to physically control and arrest a suspect after an arduous pursuit. In addition, runners need to be able to take control and execute an arrest quickly once a suspect is caught. Since growers are used to navigating the rough mountainous terrain on a daily basis, they are like running wild animals when being pursued and can and will most likely fight when caught to avoid being arrested. Runners have to be prepared for this and get them controlled and handcuffed quickly to avoid resistance.

Finally, runners have to have complete trust in the long gunners covering their movement. If one of the growers being stalked has a concealed handgun or rifle and tries to use it, the long gunners have to be able to spot this weapon quickly and deal with the threat if the runners cannot. Regardless of the runners' spotting and dealing with the threat ahead of them, the stopping power and accuracy of the 5.56 mm and 7.62 mm caliber rifles used by the long gunners is reassuring, like having angels on our shoulders. As runners we have pure confidence in the point men covering our backs, and Snake, Apache, Spag, or Ranger have never let us down.

Since the growers are usually smaller, lighter, and dressed significantly less restrictively than we are (even with our stripped-down and lighter running equipment), they have an inherent speed advantage over us.

Just as important is the grower's familiarity with the terrain and the garden layout in general. Keep in mind these criminals live at these grow sites for up to six months at a time. They are acclimated to the terrain and are used to moving across it quickly and efficiently day and night.

In addition, growers have several planned escape route trails in every grow site they work. They know every inch of their garden and have planned and practiced how to get to these escape routes quickly to avoid detection. If they hear an arrest team approaching on foot or a CAMP or other task force helicopter approaching from above, or in this case if they are running to avoid capture from pursuing operators, they can simply drop down an escape trail and may never be found. All these challenges create a need for running teams to get *extremely close* and *avoid detection* before it is too late, and to control and handcuff the growers before a sprint chase breaks out.

This is where the stalking skills of the runners, and all arrest team members for that matter, can be a great advantage to a successful catch. Runners who are not only in good physical shape but also have extensive stalking experience have a distinct advantage in catching these crafty criminals. Like Cheetah and me, operators who run routinely for physical fitness or competition purposes and have a lot of hunting experience make competent runners. Those of us who hunt practice our approach by stalking animals to get close enough to surprise and take the animal humanely, so sneaking up on a distracted grower is possible. Even without hunting experience, most wardens have had numerous training cycles or poaching cases where undetected stalking into a hide area is required.

For example, Spag does not hunt animals, yet he has excellent stalking skills. Given his years of sniper training, he has become very competent at stalking through any wooded environment. I have been paired with Spag several times as a light runner over the past few eradication seasons, and in each case I've been impressed with how silent and difficult to detect he is when moving in the woods.

Without the added weight of our hydration packs, Cheetah and I were as light as possible and ready to move. We looked at Snake for the go signal. Snake looked at us and nodded slowly, indicating that he and Spag had us covered with their rifles and we could begin our stalk. Cheetah would move up first with me following close behind. With a two-handed hold on our Glock pistols now held at a low ready position, Cheetah and I slowly stood up from our kneeling stance and silently moved down the trail. Rolling our feet heel to toe to be as quiet as possible and still be grounded and ready to shoot instantly if need be, we kept our eyes on the growers, looking for any signs of our being detected. Still focused on processing their dope, all three growers were oblivious to our presence and completely unaware they were being hunted.

Cheetah was reading the terrain in front of us perfectly as we moved down the trail. A large oak tree and some brush were between us and the growers, giving us points of cover to work with as we got closer. In the shadows of the dark canyon, we continued to glide silently toward the first tree, now less than 30 yards away from the growers. When we reached the tree we stopped for a minute to listen and again check for signs of detection. Nothing moved around us, and it was completely silent. So quiet in fact, that I could hear my heart beating rapidly from the recent adrenaline dump. My heartbeat kicked up another notch as we stalked closer to our suspects.

Moving away from the cover of the tree, Cheetah and I discovered a problem. No more brush or other concealment existed between our position and the manzanita trees the growers were working in. This left the last 20 yards of our stalk on an uphill, exposed dirt slope with nothing to hide our presence or movement. We had no choice but to continue and hope they did not notice us until it was too late.

We moved out from the cover of the tree and slowly closed the gap. Feeling uncomfortably exposed as we moved, we made the best of it, and the growers were now just 15 yards ahead. We could hear them talking clearly now, and we could see that each man was using a pair of scissors and trimming large buds off the tops of marijuana plants. Although all three men were actually facing us and we were almost at eye level now and approaching their position in the open, none of them had seen us yet. A testament to proper head-to-toe camouflage and slow movement, the growers had not identified us yet as they focused on their trimming tasks. I could not believe we were getting this close!

In general, growers are used to hearing arrest teams approaching their grow sites and escaping well before team members can see them. And if an arrest team sees growers it's usually from a long distance through heavily wooded cover that allows plenty of escape time for the growers. This is why so few growers are caught in grow operations throughout the state. Today was going to be a big surprise for this unfortunate crew.

At 10 yards everything changed. With Cheetah just 3 feet ahead of me, one of the growers, a tall, lanky man in his midtwenties, stopped talking in midsentence and froze holding a pair of scissors in one hand and a long marijuana bud in the other. Looking right at us I saw the expression on his face change from contentment to a look of total shock. His mouth dropped open and his eyes opened up as wide as silver dollars a second before he let out a distress sound to the rest of the group in Spanish. Seeing two fully camouflaged and armed operators creeping up on his crew so closely was clearly alarming.

At that moment the woods were no longer silent as chaos broke out. All three growers were now yelling, looking at us, dropping their cutting tools and marijuana buds, and jumping up to run away from their processing station. Two of the men ran directly to the south and to the right of our position through a large marijuana garden just above the trail. The youngest, tallest, and most physically fit grower who had spotted us first was turning to go in the opposite direction. He was starting to run east and away from Cheetah and me beyond the processing trees.

Before the grower completed his turn to run away from us, Cheetah had read his escape perfectly and was already picking up speed in his direction. Realizing he was going to be the fastest of the three, Cheetah committed us to this man and told me, "We're on the tall fast one! Let the rest of the team deal with the other two guys!" A good call, and now the chase was on.

This guy was fast, really fast, and as agile as a scared blacktail deer running through the woods. Cheetah and I were in full stride and sprinting as fast as possible in pursuit through a large marijuana grow that extended along the ridgeline for the next 100 yards. After about 40 yards I could see that we were gaining on him. The grower was in full stride running past large marijuana plants and jumping over the smaller ones as we chased. Thirty yards away . . . now 20 yards away . . .

At the end of the garden was a large brush pile, built up like a wall around the grow, about 20 feet long by 6 feet deep and 6 feet wide. Made up of manzanita, coyote brush, and other brush cuttings, this pile had been placed there by the growers when they cleared all vegetation from the garden site to make room for their high-dollar crop. Past this brush pile was a steep downhill slope covered in heavy brush and poison oak. Cheetah and I both knew that if the grower made it past the brush pile and down into the abyss of the brushy canyon below, we would most likely lose him. We had to get him in the next few seconds over the next 30 yards, or it was over.

Just 10 yards away from us now, the grower reached the edge of the brush pile and tried to jump over it. Fortunately for us he did not clear the pile and instead of landing past it and continuing to run, he fell into the pile up to his neck. With only his head and part of his shoulders and neck visible above the pile, the grower looked like a man trapped in a quicksand pit and slowly sinking. Within a second of being caught in the brush, though, the man started to climb and tear his way out of the pile. He was almost clear of the pile and free to run again when Cheetah and I made our move.

True to his nickname because of his speed, Cheetah jumped through the air across the top of the brush pile while I covered his back. Just as the grower was breaking free of the pile, Cheetah landed on the grower's head putting one hand on his neck and the other on his left shoulder. A second later, I took the leap as well, landing on the grower's right shoulder. Between the two of us, he was not going anywhere.

As we pulled the man out of the brush pile and placed him in handcuffs, I could see Markos moving up to our position, covering us with his M14. Markos had gotten to us quickly considering all the gear he was carrying including the big battle rifle. Being escorted in handcuffs now and looking at the muzzle of Markos's M14 had taken the rest of the fight out of this guy. This grower was now compliant.

The team was elated. The light runner concept had worked for the first time since its inception on our first operation of the season. And while we did not catch the other two growers, the cell phone in the pocket of the man we did catch was highly valuable. Numerous contacts related to that location's cultivation conspiracy were discovered on the phone giving us a better idea of the depth of the network associated with operations in this area.

We walked the grower back into the center of the garden we had just chased him through and waited for the rest of the team. After bringing the point team and QRF together, both teams cleared all the trails around and in the garden site, finding and clearing the camp and kitchen area along the way. In addition, team members located all water sources for the garden before it was time to eradicate and bring in the CAMP team to assist. Since the hike out of that steep canyon with a prisoner would be challenging, and because we had CAMP help on this day, the grower would be taken out of the woods on a stokes basket on a long line under the helicopter.

Back in the center of the garden, and with the prisoner now being guarded by Rails, Cheetah and I started to cut down and eradicate marijuana plants. Looking at the thick understory of brush around us, we both knew we needed to cut out a landing zone for CAMP's helicopter to safely lift and pull out our numerous net loads of dope.

Still excited over our recent catch, Cheetah and I located a site and began cutting brush for a landing zone. Needing a blade capable of cutting through thick manzanita tree bases, I borrowed Cheetah's Gerber machete. This blade is razor sharp and perfect for cutting down thick-stalked marijuana plants and small trees in a garden. With Cheetah below my position, I began using his machete to cut branches in the way of our landing zone when my right foot lost its footing and I slipped backward. As I slipped, still swinging the blade down to the base of the brush I was cutting, I felt the blade overshoot the branch and graze the side of my right leg just below my knee. Not feeling anything unusual, I ignored it and resumed cutting brush. Seconds later I looked down and noticed my camo BDU pants had a tear in them about 3 inches wide where the blade had grazed my leg. In addition to the slice in my pants, I could see a wet and dark pool soaking the fabric around the slice, and it was getting bigger. Now it registered. I had just cut myself more severely than a graze. Not good.

When checking the wound, I learned I had cut a 3-inch gash across the side of my leg at a forty-five-degree angle toward the bone.

I had not hit bone, fortunately, but had cut deeply into the skin and tissue and was now bleeding heavily. Damn it! What a rookie move. I told Cheetah what happened and called out for medical assistance.

Fortunately, Doc was only 50 yards away when he heard my call for help and was at my location within seconds. After assessing the wound, Doc told me the cut was deep and would require several stitches and a good cleaning to avoid infection. Given the fact that the blade was dirty, infection was a major concern.

Doc had to stop the bleeding quickly, so he took out a packet of QuikClot, an anticoagulant powder developed for gunshot wounds in combat. Used extensively by our military forces, this powder poured directly into any bleeding wound, no matter how severe, works quickly at reacting with blood to stop the bleeding and temporarily seal the wound. After pouring the powder into my cut, the wound heated up slightly but not to a point of discomfort. As advertised, within seconds the bleeding stopped. After this, Doc wrapped the wound in a gauze dressing and told me I was done working for the day and needed to get short-hauled out of the garden and driven to an emergency room for secondary care as soon as possible.

I felt terrible. It was getting hot and our teams were just now starting to eradicate. This was the hardest part of the day on these missions—when the real work began—and I was now out of the action and unable to help the team for at least the rest of that day.

Within a few minutes, the CAMP chopper was hovering overhead, and with my short haul harness checked and secured under my tactical gear, I was on the line being lifted and transported to the command post above the garden on Montebello Road.

When touching down on the ground under the bird, I released the line from my harness and walked to my patrol truck before taking off all my gear. Then I jumped in my patrol truck and began the drive out of the foothills to a hospital.

Once at the hospital, I was rushed into the nurse's station and was treated immediately. The medical staff at St. Louise Hospital were great. After an hour of cleaning the QuikClot out of my wound, a very skilled nurse sewed me up with seventeen well-placed stitches. I would have a slight scar across that part of my leg as a trophy. I pointed out to the nurse that my team was still in the hills eradicating in the heat of the day and I wanted to get back to the command post and help however possible. The nurse told me in no uncertain terms that I was done for the day. Afraid to ask but needing to, I inquired about the next day's mission and stressed how critical it was that I work it with the rest of the team. She thought about it and agreed, provided I was not on my feet more than half of the following day. She also told me to monitor the cut constantly throughout the morning and stop working immediately if the wound opened up or began to hurt. I smiled and thanked her for looking after me before giving her a big hug and leaving the hospital.

I met up with Markos and Cheetah late that afternoon back at my house. Both of them looked beat and told me that the CAMP helicopter had found several more gardens around our chase site after I was extracted. The team had been short-hauling to other grow sites with CAMP all afternoon and eradicated a bunch more dope. By the day's end, the teams had eradicated over 25,000 plants, a big haul for us on any given day.

Exhausted, all three of us discussed the day's events over dinner. It had been a good day filled with excitement, success, and, as usual, some unpredictable surprises. We were in bed early that night, slightly anxious knowing the next day was another operation we all needed to be fresh and focused for—a grow site with another good trail to stalk and chase down growers in an area known for guns and violence. We would be ready.

CHAPTER 4

Bohlman Road Gunfight: Déjà Vu Above the Quiet Suburbs

The kingdom of heaven suffers violence, and violent men take it by force.
—Matthew 11:12 (New American Standard Bible)

I woke up in a fog. Peeling my eyes open slowly, I saw it was 4:20 a.m. Even groggy I had to laugh at the irony of these numbers. Four-twenty is the common date throughout the cultivation culture when grow operations begin and the date when growers start putting plants in the ground. It is also the date of "Weed Day," when people assemble in public and smoke marijuana to call for legalization. I did not think of this when I set the alarm the night before, but wondered now if it was some subconscious reminder.

It was time to get up and get ready for the second part of a two-day eradication operation with our MET. Still tired from the previous day on Montebello Road, I slowly leaned over and silenced the demon alarm.

In a flood of awareness, everything from yesterday came back to me. The foot chase with Cheetah, barely catching the grower as he made a final dash to escape from the brush pile, and then slicing my leg open later that morning. Now it hit me, and panic ran through my mind. Was my leg okay? Would I be able to work today?

I pulled back the covers and did a couple of leg bends and

checked the bandage wrap around my wound. No bleeding through the night and, surprisingly, no soreness. The stitches were holding fine. I was going to work with the rest of the team today.

At 5:00 a.m., after wolfing down fruit and drinking lots of water to thoroughly hydrate myself, Markos, Cheetah, and I drove to the north-western foothills of Santa Clara County. This grow was in the same mountain range, but a bit south of the operation the day before.

Above the quiet, calm, and affluent community of Saratoga, today's mission would take us into another steep canyon, this time on Midpeninsula Open Space property. Alarmingly close to a wooded community of owners of custom-built houses, this grow site was just like the day before—perfectly positioned and well hidden with an excellent year-round water source. And like so many other grow sites we found throughout the Santa Clara County foothills, it was insidiously located right under the nose of so many people.

The MET assembled at the top of Bohlman Road in a large open meadow—lots of room for a landing zone for the CAMP helicopter and all our vehicles. Anticipating the heat later in the day, we all parked our patrol trucks under some shade trees on the edge of the meadow before gearing up, conducting a weapons and radio check, and met in the center of the field to go over the operations plan for the day.

Snake was the lead on today's raid and would be conducting the briefing. When I joined Snake in the center of the meadow I noticed that two operators from our point team were missing: Spag and Apache. I was disappointed. Teamwork is what makes these details happen.

Seconds later my spirits were quickly elevated when I saw a familiar face in the mix of team members at the briefing spot. With his face painted dark, wearing his trademark fleece beanie cap, and carrying a nicely subdued, fully automatic M4 carbine, Ranger looked as prepared as always.

A full-time patrol deputy, field training officer, and entry gunner on the sheriff's office SERT team, Ranger's level head, humble demeanor, and constant humorous and upbeat personality made him a pleasure to work with. Because of his full-time patrol assignment, Ranger was on loan periodically throughout the year to assist our team whenever possible, which usually turned out to be a handful of scouting missions and arrest and eradication details throughout the year.

His code name was no accident. A U.S. Army Ranger throughout the 1990s who saw action in hotspots around the globe during that time, he was no stranger to special operations in the woods. Highly skilled in land navigation, map reading, stalking and field craft, Ranger was a natural hunter and oftentimes our point man on the toughest, most physically and mentally demanding scouting missions the MET had conducted over the last three years. There was no quit in this guy.

That day's plan was a mirror image of the one the day before. The hike should be almost the same distance as the previous day's. Two teams would stalk down on the grower's trail to the grow site. Once again, we would be fielding a point team that included a pair of light runners (Cheetah and me) who would attempt to stalk close enough to catch suspects. In addition, we would have a secondary team, a QRF, 50 to 80 yards behind the point team to support and assist as needed.

Woody was working with us that day and, like the day before, would work with the QRF to assist our team. Our responsibility was to clear the garden of all safety threats and then have the CAMP team come in to assist with eradication, hopefully no later than around 9:00 a.m. That would be plenty of time to get in and scour the grow for bad guys before eradicating the crop in the heat of the day.

The day's operation included another element: members of the press. The local NBC affiliate's investigative reporting team was on site to cover the MET throughout the day's operation. For obvious safety reasons, the press team would not go into the grow site until it was cleared of all threats. Once the garden was secure and the area declared safe, Rails and I would hike back up to the command post before escorting the press team down to the grow site. The reporters were planning to cover and explain the inner workings of an illegal cultivation operation at the peak of harvest time and the dangers to public safety posed by violent men who were exploiting a beautiful natural area with ruthless disregard for wildlife or humans.

The environmental criminality and wildlife resource destruction in these cultivation sites was very important to California's Department of Fish and Game. Up until the last few years, the public and other law enforcement agencies were unaware of what was going on; no one realized how much wildlife habitat, stream bed, and water quality destruction takes place in these cultivation sites. Media exposure with photographs or video coverage of the damage can engender manpower, equipment, and personnel support for resource restoration from many groups in the public and in law enforcement. Garnering such support has become the second battlefront.

Snake's briefing went smoothly. Most of that day's players were involved in the raid the day before and knew the drill and their roles well. Given the location and the high probability of growers with guns in the woods below us, safety was emphasized. When it was my turn to brief, I reminded everyone to stay focused and to expect the unexpected. As we have been too often reminded of in the past, *anything* can happen out there.

We fell into formation for the assault. Ranger was on point with Snake this time. Cheetah and I were right behind them with Rails and Markos again covering us in the number five and six positions. Woody was overseeing the second team, the QRF, behind us at a comfortable interval to keep things as quiet as possible in the woods.

We conducted a quick radio check, and Snake looked back giving all of us the thumbs-up sign. One by one we nodded and returned the gesture, indicating we were ready to roll.

The trail into the canyon was strikingly similar to the footpath the day before. Well worn, quiet, and clear of leaf litter and other debris, it was ideal for stalking growers. Numerous fresh footprints indicated heavy grower traffic, showing growers going up and down on a regular basis and implying signs of harvest time. The heavy foot traffic also told us we could run into a grower anywhere on the trail or we could even be threatened by someone coming down the trail behind us once both teams were off the road and in the woods. Snake picked up on this immediately and quietly related it to the rest of our point team. On full alert, we slipped into stalking mode and descended down the trail, ready for anything.

Because of the well-worn trail, the forty-five-minute hike down to the grow site went smoothly and quietly.

Rolling my feet slowly forward with my attention focused on the trail ahead, I felt anxious with a tingling sensation throughout my injured leg. This was déjà vu from Sierra Azul in 2005—something was not right. The woods were too quiet. There was no animal movement or even birds chirping and foraging in the area. The hair on the back of my neck stood up as memories of the ambush and Mojo's injuries from three years before flashed in my mind. With situational awareness at a maximum, we moved slowly down the trail scanning carefully in all directions.

Snake and Ranger stopped suddenly ahead of us. In a collapsing domino effect, Cheetah and I stopped as well before Markos and Rails followed suit. After about thirty seconds of imitating a statue with my eyes locked down the trail, I see Snake slowly raise his rifle and look through his electronic optic.

A few seconds later Snake lowered his rifle. Maintaining his focus on what was ahead, Snake slowly raised his left hand and showed our team's tracking signal for marijuana plants. This meant that he had seen plants ahead of us and we were close to the garden.

I slowly raised my pocket binoculars to my eyes. About 30 yards away and past some small oak trees and thick brush was the start of a large, lush, green marijuana garden. The plants were laid out in symmetrical rows and looked mature and ready to harvest. The plants extended as far as I could see. This was a big one. Thick sticky buds topped most all the plants that were visible. Harvest time was happening now, and fortunately it did not look like the growers had processed the dope and got it out of the woods for sale yet. Once the rest of our point team knew what was ahead, Snake and Ranger started moving us slowly toward the garden.

After another 30 yards of stalking, we were now on the northeastern edge of the crop with the trail ahead of us. Numerous rows of marijuana plants were to our right and downhill extending as far as the eye could see. The trail took a ninety-degree turn to the right and continued downhill through the plantation.

Located directly east of the trail bend, a large water diversion had been set up by the growers to impound creek water. The diversion was made up of black plastic sheeting that lined the creek channel. Using chopped-down tree branches for structural support, the growers had made an ingenious, albeit highly damaging, makeshift pond. As a result of this impoundment, all downstream water flow was cut off, killing all aquatics and other wildlife species that relied on this channel for survival throughout the dry months of the year, an all-too-typical destructive by-product of these grow sites.

As the four of us up front reached the bend in the trail and started moving downhill, we all froze simultaneously. My heart skipped a beat and adrenaline surged throughout me as I saw two growers, dressed in dark earth-tone colors, walking through the garden ahead of us about 40 yards away and oblivious to our presence. We could hear them talking in Spanish as they moved slowly through the rows of marijuana plants. Both appeared to be patrolling the garden as opposed to working in it, which was alarming. All four of us slowly kneeled down on the ground and froze as we covered the men's movement with our weapons. The two men continued moving downhill through the plantation and disappeared.

Snake was just starting to get up and lead us after the two men when suddenly he and Ranger snapped their rifles up and aimed them into the upper edge of the garden. Without saying a word, Cheetah and I dropped back to the ground and slowly slipped our backpacks off. With our Glock pistols at the low ready, we knew a grower was somewhere ahead of us in the garden and close by. Cheetah and I were in full alert mode as we watched and waited to see who was in range of being chased down and just a few seconds from being caught.

The grower had no idea we were on the trail ahead of him as he bounded between rows of waist-high marijuana plants. All four of us had turned to our right and were now kneeling down frozen and facing the grower head on. Snake and Ranger had their AR15s shouldered and were looking for weapons on the man as he approached our position, just 25 yards away and closing. Dressed in blue jeans, a drab T-shirt, and a baseball cap, the thin and wiry man continued toward us, still oblivious to the four operators waiting so close ahead.

Snake and Ranger were positioned below and out of our way on the edge of the trail. This allowed Cheetah and me a straight shot at our suspect if a foot chase started. At this rate, the grower was going to walk right into our team, still not identifying us in our camouflage.

With my injured leg feeling surprisingly strong, I leaned slightly forward, placing the majority of my weight on my left foot in front of me while simultaneously planting my right foot behind me, preparing my body for the imminent sprint. Just a few feet ahead of me and true to his code name, my partner was crouched and moving up and down slowly like a big predator cat getting ready to tackle his prey. He raised and bent his arms along the sides of his chest, and continued to spring up and down slowly, preparing for his sprint just seconds away. Excitement ripped through us as the grower closed the gap, now just 20 yards away.

When the man reached the 15-yard mark, Cheetah and I were half a second from breaking concealment and blasting forward to tackle him. Before doing so and barely in time to stop our pursuit, we heard Ranger whisper frantically, "He's got a long gun slung on his right shoulder!" This statement immediately changed the plan for what would happen next. Cheetah and I raised our Glock pistols on target toward the grower as we realized no chase or tackle was going to happen now. Not with a firearm on the suspect. Thank heaven for Ranger's attentive eyes!

Within a second of Ranger's observation, and with the gunman now "danger close" at only 10 yards away, Snake identified us to the suspect, "Police! Stop and put your hands up!" The man's reaction was surreal and unexpected. The grower stopped in his tracks. His eyes widened in shock for just a second before his expression turned vicious. The gunman's brow tightened, his eyes squinted, and the expression on his face turned from shock to anger and we could all see what was about to happen. Even with four guns trained on him, he was not going to back down.

Lasting only a few seconds, the actions of the felon dictated our response. With that scowl on his face, the grower swung the shotgun toward our team. Our hearts were pounding now with anger and shock, and just half a second away from pressing the trigger on our pistols, Cheetah and I heard a single, loud, high-pitched crack ring out and echo deep in the canyon. The grower wailed out a long and loud, "Aigh!!" as a single .223 caliber, 64-grain power point bullet ripped through the center of his chest.

Gripping his chest frantically as if stung by a bee, the grower buckled and bent over for a second, before recovering and continuing to stand and face the trail. Snake had hit the gunman with a single shot, making a perfect center-of-mass hit to his sternum, attempting to incapacitate him permanently. But the fight was not over yet.

When the gunman attempted to raise his shotgun on us once again, we defended ourselves and the resulting cacophony of two AR15s firing simultaneously in rapid succession at close range was deafening as Snake and Ranger shot at the attacking felon on the trail. After multiple hits from both operators, the gunfire ceased. The gunman had dropped to the trail and now no longer moved.

I was surprised when just seconds after the last AR15 rounds were fired, I saw the familiar sight of an M14 flash hider and barrel moving past the right side of my face as Markos went past me to fill in and add cover to the fight. Feeling his hand on my right shoulder as this happened and hearing him say, "On your six, Trailblazer, and moving to you!" was comforting. Markos had heard so much gunfire up ahead, and thinking his teammates were in major trouble, he wasted no time moving up to get in the fight and help.

Realizing the gunman was being handled by Snake and Ranger, Cheetah and I aimed our pistols farther downhill and scanned deeper into the grow, while Markos did the same with his M14. The two other growers witnessed earlier were still out there, ignored but not forgotten.

We looked up just in time to see both growers running down-hill. They apparently wanted nothing to do with that action and were leaving their buddy to fend for himself.

The taller of the two growers towered well above the chest-high budded plants. And looking back in our direction as he ran, the grower appeared to be carrying a long gun over his left shoulder. The second man, much shorter than the first, was not looking at anything except the path in front of him, clearly just wanting to get out of the area quickly.

Once we were sure the gunman was not going to move again, Snake conducted a sit-rep (situation report), having everyone call out their names and say if they were "up" or not ("up" means you are operational with no problems or injuries and good to go).

Immediately following the sit-rep, Snake radioed the QRF, already close to us and just a few yards behind on the trail, to come up and cover. Wasting no time and knowing we had two more growers on the run, Cheetah and I quickly told Snake what we had seen and what direction the growers were headed in. I told Snake we knew their direction of travel and could cover him to the east if he wanted to head downhill and cut their escape trail below, while at the same time we would be clearing that side of the garden. Snake agreed, and before the three of us moved out, he directed a secondary team to work down through the western edge to check and clear that side of the grow. Ranger, Markos, and Rails made up that team and were already moving before Snake finished conveying his plan.

With a dead gunman in the middle of the garden, we now had a crime scene to deal with. Not only did we have to clear the immedi-ate area of all threats, we also had to do so without disturbing any-thing critical to the impending shooting investigation.

Woody was now standing next to Cheetah and me. Calmly and

decisively, he directed Doc, along with some long gun support, to check the gunman's vital signs. After a minute of checking, Doc looked up and slowly shook his head. This man was not getting up ever again.

Woody was in high gear overseeing things at the shooting scene. While our security teams were moving through the rest of the garden looking for more growers, Woody was delineating a perimeter around the gunman's body to help preserve evidence.

Woody also directed other members of the QRF to look for and clear a feasible landing zone close enough to the shooting site for a helicopter to insert and extract personnel as needed. Over the next two days, SWAT and tracking team operators, crime scene investigators, and other officials would all need to be at the shooting site to do their business. Hiking all the investigator teams into the area like we did earlier was not an option. Doing so was too dangerous and time consuming. As a result of the day's events so far, our CAMP team would not be eradicating as planned. Instead, they would be helping to get numerous officers in and out of the rugged and practically inaccessible crime scene.

As Woody handled logistics at the shooting site, Snake, Cheetah, and I were clearing and tracking on the trail below. With slow and stealthy movement no longer necessary, we went quickly downhill along the eastern edge of the garden looking for the two fleeing growers.

When we reached the bottom of the garden where the main trail ended, we found ourselves standing on the edge of a heavily wooded and steep ridgeline. Through the treeline below us, we could see completely across the canyon to the next ridge. Covered in multiple canopies of trees and other vegetation as far as the eye could see, it became clear that tracking these guys now was going to be very difficult. Just like the dense cover across the canyon, the woods below us were no different. With a rocky creek in the bottom of the canyon between both ridgelines, and with the men's escape trails so well established, tracking them was going to be a challenge. The three of us kneeled down and covered the canyon below with our weapons. We could not go any farther and still safely cover the perimeter of the garden, now an urgent necessity given the gunfight. We held our positions and waited to hear from the other perimeter team and what they discovered.

Within a few minutes, Rails was on the radio giving us an update. Our three partners on that team had found and cut the tracks from the fleeing growers on the western edge of the plantation. The trio then tracked them to the bottom of the garden and farther down the canyon to a large camp and kitchen area. When Rails described the camp, the urgency in his voice was obvious.

The camp and kitchen area were big enough to house and supply eight to ten growers at least, and the amount of tracks in the camp verified this. The reality that several more armed growers were moving around the garden near us to monitor our actions was unnerving. Given one man's violence already, the possibility of gunmen hiding close and just waiting for us to leave to reclaim their crop was on our minds. This was not an uncommon practice in these cultivation operations where the pressure from above to protect and deliver the crop at all costs is intense. Worse yet was the possibility of an ambush from anywhere in the dense woods around the crop. Still on high alert, we maintained our guard as both our teams monitored our perimeter positions.

Back at the shooting site, Woody had things running smoothly. Just like the Sierra Azul gunfight in 2005, the SERT team had been mobilized as soon as the command staff in the valley knew about the shooting.

Before any crime scene investigation staff or other investigators could be safely delivered to the shooting scene, operators skilled in providing security at the shooting site were needed first. SERT members were now arriving at the command post and within the hour would start to be short-hauled into the grow via the CAMP helicopter.

As members of the morning's QRF team filled in our perimeter spots, Snake, Cheetah, and I moved back uphill into the center of the grow site. With Woody, Ranger, Rails, and Markos all present at the newly cut landing zone, the six of us debriefed what we had found and what needed to happen next. The shooting site and garden were secure, and we had fresh tracks of not only the two fleeing growers but also several other growers as well to follow with a fresh tracking team.

By that time, Apache and Spag—two of the best operators and skilled man trackers—were both available and responded when their SERT pagers went off. We knew they would be the first ones lowered into the grow by the helicopter on the short-haul line to assist us. Surely upset that they were not on the mission that morning to help, both would be chomping at the bit to bag some growers.

Fifteen minutes later, we could hear CAMP's Jet Ranger helicopter approaching us. The chopper appeared through the tree canopy 200 feet above. And on the line 100 feet below the sleek bird, two operators were suspended in the air with their AR15 carbines at their sides and at the ready. Sure enough it was Spag and Apache!

As soon as they were on the ground I grabbed Apache and gave him a bear hug before doing the same to Spag. They both smiled at all of us before Apache said, "Sorry, guys. I feel terrible for not being here this morning. The one day all season we could not make the operation and you guys get into it without us!" All of us did our best to quell our frustration, as we all knew it bothered both of them tremendously.

During a critical incident like this, a feeling of loss is common when core members of the team are not present. And because of everyone's dedication and loyalty to the team, the guilt of not being present when your brother operators are in battle can be unsettling. Unlike the 2005 shooting, though, no one on our side was hurt this time, which made things a little easier to handle for the team members not present. And because those of us on the team who were trained in fugitive man-tracking tactics could not stay on scene to track growers, having Spag and Apache there for that was a godsend.

Snake and I briefed Spag and Apache on exactly what had occurred throughout the morning and where we had last seen the growers on the run. As we were briefing, Markos called out from a few yards below, "Nice, one of the growers did not want to carry his pistol on the run!" We saw Markos pointing down toward the ground in front of him. On the dirt next to a tall budding marijuana plant was a German P-38 replica 9 mm automatic pistol. Shortly, we all learned the pistol's magazine was full of 9 mm hollow-point ammunition—the kind used by law enforcement agencies to stop people.

Throughout the next hour, more SERT operators were lowered into the shooting site two at a time. Once the last pair of operators was on the ground, Spag and Apache picked four to join them as a tracking team. The remaining team members were directed to take up security positions throughout the garden, reinforcing the shooting site.

Knowing that every minute that passed added exponentially to the difficulty of finding the fleeing felons, Spag and Apache's tracking team was on the move immediately. Moving down the ridge to cut tracks in the gunman's camp, the team would spend the rest of the afternoon tracking the growers exhaustively in midday temperatures approaching 100 degrees.

For the next two hours, Cheetah, Markos, and I secured the shooting site, while the rest of the point and QRF team members provided some type of security throughout the grow. After what seemed like forever, the CAMP pilot radioed our teams to be ready for extraction within the next fifteen minutes. This was great news, as all of us were growing restless and impatient sitting in the grow. With so much more shooting investigation responsibilities still ahead of us that day, we all needed to get out of the woods.

Markos and I were first on the short-haul line for extraction, and once we were pulled off the ground and into the air past the canopy of trees, I let out a sigh of relief. As the grow site became smaller below us and the urban sprawl of Silicon Valley became visible to the east, I felt alive and proud of my team's performance and the men in it. Everyone was safe and performed well today.

I felt fortunate Markos and Cheetah were involved in today's operation. Having not been involved in any gunfights before, both game wardens had done a terrific job of dealing with the threat safely and decisively. Like the rest of the point team members, their bravery was exemplary.

I made a fist and bumped it against my partner's before looking into Markos's eyes and telling him over the roar of the wild ride. "Good work today, brother! Can't tell you how good it felt to feel you at my back and see your rifle passing me up for support!"

Markos smiled and replied back, "No problem, bud. When I heard that second volley of shots, it sounded like a war zone down there! I thought all four of you had to be taking and returning fire with several shooters, and I couldn't let you guys face it alone!"

Dragged through the air at 100 mph, with the hot midday wind ripping across our faces, we were excited and enjoying the short-haul ride as I reflected on the morning's events. After the ambush of the 2005 shooting and the frustration of having a gunman who slipped away, this day was an affirmation of things going right in a limited-option situation. Unlike the events of August 5, 2005, no one on the MET had been hurt, and the bad guys had lost this fight. That was a good feeling

As a result of the shooting, the once small command post was now filled to the brim with personnel. The meadow below us was covered with emergency response vehicles from all over the county. Tactical team member transport, medical response, forensic, and numerous agency patrol vehicles of all types littered the entire span of the grass field below us. And even from 200 hundred feet above the landing zone, we could see several Fish and Game patrol vehicles other than our own parked in the command post.

Less than 30 seconds later, Markos and I were on the ground, detaching the long line from our short-haul harnesses, and giving the "all clear" signal to the chopper above. We ran to the edge of the landing zone where a sheriff's office detective greeted us before directing us to a portable shade tent. Along the walk to the tent, I saw my captain and district patrol chief along with several neighboring wardens standing by the medical support vehicles and watching us move through the crowd. I gave a "thumbs-up" sign indicating we were all okay, and Chief Carmela and Captain Huck both smiled and returned the "thumbs-up". Their presence was immediately calming as we knew we had plenty of department support on scene. And they were all relieved and happy to see us on the ground safe and sound. After quickly updating the chief and the captain, we were rushed away to a shade tent next to the landing zone.

Under the tent we saw some of the other members of that morning's QRF team, as we were directed to portable chairs. The shade tent was surrounded by yellow caution tape. With all the agency personnel, vehicles, and equipment surrounding us, being under and within the perimeter of that boundary and the shade tent was surreal. We felt like temporarily quarantined space explorers being screened for health and safety reasons after a shuttle mission. The Sierra Azul command post three years prior did not have this setup, which was designed to speed things up when doing medical and mental health screening, and it was definitely an improvement over the shooting command post in 2005.

Several different SWAT doctors and psychologists checked us for trauma on all levels. Each one of us had a doctor, and that attention was reassuring after such an unpredictable morning. Following our checkups, the food arrived! Given the fact that neither Markos, Cheetah, nor I had to press our gun triggers this time, we did not have to wait to eat before having our blood drawn. When the fresh sandwiches, chips, fruit, and cold drinks arrived, I suddenly realized it had been eight hours since we last ate. At that point in the operation, anything edible would have tasted like a gourmet meal.

After lunch, those of us on the point team were paired with different sheriff's office investigators to drive back to the headquarters office in San José to complete our interviews. Now that I was familiar with this process, my anxiety level lowered. All of us just wanted to get in and out of the office as soon as possible. After an hour of navigating through a sea of agency vehicles and winding our way out of the Saratoga foothills, we parked at the sheriff's office headquarters in downtown San José. A few minutes later, we were escorted upstairs to a large conference room in the investigations division to wait for our interviews.

Because the three of us from Fish and Game had not fired our weapons, we would not have to wait long for the interview process. Snake and Ranger would be the last two operators to be questioned given their trigger time.

Markos and Cheetah were the first to debrief. They were done within forty-five minutes, and I was next. Between our interviews, I saw Chief Carmela and Captain Huck walking down the hallway toward the conference room. Both had left the command post as soon as we did so they could be present at the sheriff's office through this process. It was calming to see them both, and talking with them briefly before my interview helped.

My interview was quick considering the morning's drama, and within thirty minutes, I was back at the conference room talking with Markos, Cheetah, and the rest of the MET members from the morning's mission.

When all three of us were finished with our interviews, Chief Carmela told us the Critical Incident Response Team members had arrived. Just as they were in the 2005 shooting, Jonesy and Lynn were not only peer counselors for this type of event but friends of all three of us as well. As a result, talking to both of them was comfortable and helpful given the day's events. Like me, Jonesy had been in an officer-involved shooting incident several years before. Understanding exactly what a brother officer was going through made Jonesy and Lynn welcome faces at the end of a long, stressful day. And their support was appreciated.

The five of us talked for close to an hour before leaving the room. Only after talking with command staff from my department and the sheriff's office, did we realize we were finally done for the day. After some quick supportive talks with members from our team, we left the sheriff's office and headed home. With no more operations in the immediate future (and Snake and Ranger on routine two-week administrative leave following their involvement in the shooting) we were finished chasing growers and eradicating dope at least for the next two weeks. Given the events of the last two days especially, we all needed the break. With most wardens in my area working twelve-hour days this time of year and covering at least two patrol districts due to vacancies, a lull in the action after today's events was especially necessary.

That night at a restaurant, seated around a large table with Markos, Cheetah, and some of my family members, we could really unwind and talk. We celebrated survival and fellowship and savored what was really important in our lives—those loved ones around us that night and on the home front. They are what matters most. The sacrifice, concern, and endless support they provide gives us the strength to keep fighting this war. I smiled as I watched everyone's faces as the day's events were described and the conversation continued. Laughter was the key ingredient that night, and everyone was happy.

Before leaving the restaurant and heading back home to clean weapons and gear and get some much needed sleep, I said a silent prayer. I thanked God for once again keeping us safe through another chaotic and deadly day, for bringing the right people together at the right time that morning, and for the amazing people in our lives we are fortunate to return home to.

CHAPTER 5

Day Mountain and the Arroyo Hondo: The Toughest Find Yet

The credit belongs to the man in the arena, whose face is marred by dust and sweat and blood, who strives valiantly . . . who at best knows in the end the triumph of high achievement, and who at worst, if he fails, at least fails while daring greatly, so that his place shall never be with those cold and timid souls who have never known neither victory nor defeat.

—TEDDY ROOSEVELT

My right foot throbbed as I ran down the rocky trail, slowly closing the distance to the fleeing gunman. Now past the many rows of budding marijuana plants in the garden, the chase traversed a rocky trail cut into the side of the hill. The felon was only 20 yards ahead of me as I tried to gain on his stride. Ignoring the pain in my shin from the fall on a sharp rock just seconds before, I kept running. Having lost Spag, my running partner, just seconds before to a fall of his own, I was committing a MET sin now—chasing a suspect alone.

It was harvest time, August 2008, and two years' worth of memories of working this operation flashed through my mind as I pounded ahead. This had been the most challenging garden to find over the last four years of our efforts. Bits and pieces of countless hours of reconnaissance, overflights, and investigation—all of these surfaced at light speed as I charged after the gunman. Shaking from the adrenaline throughout my body and gasping for air to fill my lungs for a little more speed, I sprinted ahead remembering how it all started two years prior.

❖

While Rails always sounded upbeat whenever we talked, this phone conversation was different. The excitement in his voice was evident, but there was more. He sounded troubled, puzzled by the big picture of what his find had uncovered. It was the most remote and insidious cultivation operation occurring in our county, and it was a rare and lucky find. It was early October 2006 and well into the end of the cultivation season. We both knew time was of the essence, and given the terrain and access difficulty, there was a lot of work ahead.

Rails immediately asked me if I was familiar with the Badger Ranch above the Arroyo Hondo River. I told him I was, having worked with the owner of that ranch on several poaching problems and game management issues in the past.

The Arroyo Hondo River, located in the mountains east of and above the city of Milpitas, is the largest and most pristine watershed in Santa Clara County. Stretching through water company property and cut off from public access, the Arroyo Hondo flows for almost 18 miles between the base of Mount Hamilton, the tallest mountain in the San Francisco Bay Area at 4,360 feet, and Calaveras Reservoir through the remotest, most rugged, and steeply wooded terrain in our county. The Badger Ranch encompasses one of several private hunting ranches.

Day Mountain contains several thousand acres of oak, pine tree, and brush woodlands along the Arroyo Hondo's eastern slopes almost 3,000 feet above the riverbed.

Given the Arroyo Hondo's remote location and rugged terrain, few if any people see or navigate through it during any given year. And up until this phone call, even with all my antipoaching work on both sides of the river over the past fifteen years, I had never hiked the whole stretch of the river, a dream of mine since I started working. This was finally going to happen for reasons I would never have guessed.

Rails told me that one of the trail cameras on the ranch had picked up something interesting just a few days before. Trail cameras are outdoor digital cameras with built-in motion sensors that remotely photograph anything moving within a set distance twenty-four hours a day. Used primarily to identify the types of animals passing through a particular area, these cameras are very helpful for hunting and game management purposes. Over the past several years, however, these cameras have become valuable in law enforcement efforts against wildlife poaching and marijuana cultivation.

When checking the photos captured on the trail cameras throughout the ranch, Jim (the Badger Ranch owner) was shocked and alarmed by what he found. In the middle of a series of wildlife pictures showing deer feeding and moving down one of his dirt roads was a picture of two men clearly up to no good. In the picture, both men were dressed in camouflage clothing and carrying olive-colored military cargo bags full of supplies. More careful examination of this photo revealed that the bags were likely full of marijuana cultivation tools and food supplies, and that these two men were part of a large cultivation operation somewhere north of the camera's location.

When I heard this, I was instantly as excited as Rails and asked him to e-mail the picture for me to examine. I grew even more intrigued when I opened the photo and examined it closely. I knew this area well; a few years before I worked and walked the road where this picture was taken. As I zoomed in on certain sections of the image and scanned the details in the photo, my mind was already in overdrive thinking about possible destinations for these two men.

I noticed how heavy and full the growers' packs appeared. And besides their heavy packs, both men were carrying drinking and food supplies in their hands, clearly bringing in as much goods as they could carry. This late in the growing season meant one thing only. These growers were moving supplies in to assist in the harvest and processing phase of the operation. This is a time when more workers than ever are needed to process the dope and get it out of the woods as quickly as possible to avoid detection.

The photo was also showing us that a grow this remote this late in the season had to be big. In general, October is late to be harvesting and processing a grow, given the rapid approach of winter rains. This was another indication that this big grow had been in the harvest and processing phase for quite some time now.

Photos like this are rare at best, as growers moving into and out of any grow site are seldom caught on camera. We had just hit the jackpot!

As I continued to examine the picture and talk with Rails, something else caught my eye. The camera captured the men in the early morning hours when the sun was just cresting the eastern foothills and casting shadows across the road. I got the chills for a minute when I suddenly realized the effort these men were putting into just getting to the grow site wherever it may be. From the last possible dropoff point by vehicle, these growers had already hiked across two private ranches covering several thousand acres. They had traveled almost 6 miles when the picture was taken and still had to go at least one more mile just to get off the Badger Ranch and drop into the Arroyo Hondo drainage to reach the garden. These guys were tough to have hiked that far carrying all those heavy supplies. And they must have started their hike in the middle of the night before to make it this far by sunrise. Rails and I had no doubt the garden was in the Hondo drainage somewhere, but where exactly was just a guess.

This was for certain a skilled and tough crew of growers working this operation. The terrain challenges alone were the toughest we had seen in the county to date, and any group that worked this hard to run a grow operation in such a remote place surely knew its game. We already predicted that this one was camouflaged thoroughly, as were the men working it. And another chill ran down my neck as I realized this crew was surely dangerous and packing guns. This was an operation an organization would want to see succeed and reap profits from year after year without being compromised because of the sheer logistical difficulty in keeping it operational. Like Sierra Azul, a grow like this would be defended violently with firearms.

The photo was already four days old and time was critical if we wanted to find the plantation before winter set in. Rails agreed. Harvest time was over and the garden most likely abandoned by now, but we still had a chance to find it and work it next season.

Our team had suspected for a while that a large cultivation operation was taking place somewhere in the Arroyo Hondo drainage. We knew that we just had to get lucky and find it. The area was too perfect for a grow—good annual water, great sunlight throughout the day, and steep, rugged, and remote terrain. Given that a huge grow operation containing almost 50,000 plants had been eradicated in the river drainage in 2000, the MET team figured that a cartel group moving back into the region was long past due. Remotely located and virtually undetectable, the cultivation had probably been going on for several years now.

The morning after that phone conversation, Snake, Rails, Jordan, and I were on the Badger Ranch studying the camera that had taken the unusual photo a few days before. We stood at the oak tree the camera was tethered to and examined the dirt road just to our left and west of the tree. The men had been walking on the right edge of the road, passing the camera as they hiked north. The camera location put the men on the western border of the ranch, approximately a half mile south of Day Mountain.

This answered a lot of questions. We now knew the garden was not any farther south along the Arroyo Hondo than where we stood, given the men's direction of travel indicated in the photo. This realization eliminated thousands of acres of ridgeline as a potential garden site. Without that lucky photo, we may have never known where to start looking. It also verified that this was not an amateur crew working this operation.

Because of the recent rain and the fact that the photo was already almost a week old, I was not optimistic that we would find any tracks. Regardless, we had to try, so we hiked the road past the camera for several hundred yards looking for any sign from the two men. The three of us spent half the day looking carefully for a trail off Badger Ranch and into the Arroyo Hondo that could lead to a grow. By midday we had not found anything and realized we needed to change gears.

As we drove off the ranch and started the long trip back to the San José valley below us, we talked nonstop about ways to find this grow. We all came to the same conclusion: This was not going to be an easy or a quick find given everything we had learned up to that point. And it was going to take legwork and at least a handful of long and steep hiking recons into the Arroyo Hondo river drainage. Given the tough hiking conditions in this area, and the virtually straight-up-and-down nature of these hikes, we knew we needed just the right operators in the best shape to assist.

Rapidly approaching winter with each passing day, we needed to start immediately before conditions were too poor to explore the Hondo or before the harvest was completely over.

As we made our way back to the MET office in the valley, I could tell Rails was thinking about what was next on our agenda. When he dropped me off at my patrol truck, he told me he would research the maps for that entire ridgeline and find all drainages leading into the Hondo. A good idea, I agreed, and added that if we hiked all of them over the winter and early spring months, we would probably find the grow before the next season. Snake could see the seriousness on our faces and just smiled. Realizing we were already obsessed with finding this needle in a haystack, he knew we would not let it go. Already outraged that there was a cultivation operation above the Hondo that was surely polluting and destroying precious wildlife resources at that very moment, we were all committed to working until we found the grow and ended the problem.

Before parting, the three of us decided a hike needed to take place within the next week. Eager to descend into the uncharted waters of the Arroyo Hondo, I drove out of the parking lot deep in thought about which drainage we should hike first.

A week later we were into November. Snake and Rails were able to assemble a team of six operators to assist us on our first recon hike into the Hondo. Ranger was working with us on what was going to be his toughest hike on the team to date. Our plan was to hike down the first canyon just north of where the growers had been photographed and look for water sources along the way. If we were lucky enough to find the garden, we had a large enough team to handle an arrest and eradication operation if necessary. If we did not find a water source feeding a garden as we descended the drainage, we would simply continue downhill until we reached the bank and water of the Arroyo Hondo. It was just after sunrise, and knowing that every minute of daylight counted, we wasted no time in lining up and starting the hike.

The first half of the day was slower going than we predicted because of the thickly wooded terrain. On the edge of the drainage a brush line of chemise, coyote brush, and manzanita could not be traversed without a lot of work. The brush was too thick to hike through, too low to crawl under, and too tall to step over. With no other choice, Rails took point and pushed his way through the heavy brush line, fighting the foliage step after step to gain a few feet at a time. Those of us behind Rails had a much easier time following his broken-brush trail and were grateful for his sacrifice and discomfort. For the next two hours the team covered only 100 yards, moving slowly through the wooded wall of resistance.

Finally clear of the brush line, we were all relieved to be standing on an open grass slope surrounded by small oak trees. Only 200 yards above the drainage, we moved quietly and efficiently down the canyon until we were in the middle of a small creek flowing straight downhill to feed the river below. Once in the creek, the team moved silently downstream. Looking for water lines, suspects, predators, big-game animals, and anything else unusual and wild, the MET steadily moved closer to the riverbed. Like countless other grow operations we had worked before, we knew that finding any water source above the river itself could lead us to a grow site.

By two in the afternoon, we were finally within earshot of the river below. Even before seeing the river, I could hear the roar of the high water north and upstream of our position. Sounding like fast rapids, the river's flow was loud and powerful and reminded me of past rafting trips on the Colorado River in the Grand Canyon. Certainly not the size of the Colorado, the Arroyo Hondo was nevertheless a big, powerful waterway. While much smaller in size, the isolation and inaccessibility of the Arroyo Hondo made it as remote as the Grand Canyon in many ways. And the oak trees, willow trees, river grasses, and granite river rocks below us were simply beautiful.

I smiled and felt a wave of excitement as I listened to the flowing of the river. Soothing in its distant roar, my joy increased when I realized we were actually working today and getting paid to be in such a remote, beautiful, and wild place. And while holding that thought for just a minute longer, I never dropped my guard or stopped scanning down the canyon with my rifle. Somewhere within all that beauty gunmen were ready to kill in a heartbeat to defend their agenda and destroy the surrounding environment for their criminal gain and profit. Dropping our guard in this unspoiled place was unacceptable and could get us killed instantly.

We continued down the creek, and just before reaching the grassy bank of the river Snake spotted something in the rocks below him. Holding his AR15 to his side, he bent over and picked up a three-point antler set and skull from a trophy-size blacktail buck. Lying on the ground next to some old black plastic water pipe and five-gallon buckets, the rack was the prize remnant of a deer that had been poached and killed by growers. Given the age and weathering on the antler set, it was clear this animal was killed last season or before. This told us that wherever the grow site was located, it was not new and had probably been in place for many years. We secured the rack on Snake's pack to save it from poachers before continuing on to the river's edge.

We reached a grassy beach by the water where we spent the next few minutes scanning the area carefully for any sign of movement or cultivation activity. With our situational awareness at its peak, we found no threats around us, and the team members began to relax along the river's edge. We peeled our backpacks off and sat down to cool down, hydrate, and power up with some food. After a long, steep hike down into the depths of the Hondo, it felt great to finally get the pack off my back and sit down.

For the next thirty minutes we whispered quietly and soaked in the river's beauty as we rested. Just a few feet ahead, the river flowed north and downstream. Mesmerizing with its dark pools of clean cold water, the river had a remoteness and powerful solitude unmatched by any other water body in the county. The dichotomy of the Hondo struck me again. This place was so peaceful and beautiful, yet it could be so dangerous and deadly as well because of the people exploiting it. Remembering this, we all stayed on high alert looking around us periodically for any signs of someone moving in behind us.

Once rested, we put our packs back on and slung our rifles before continuing our hike out of the canyon. Given the late hour and wanting to get out of the woods before dark, we would go no farther that day. With Ranger and me on point, we started back up the creek drainage with the rest of the MET members following behind at safe intervals.

Hiking the creek upstream was challenging and slow going at best. With the creek still flowing strongly this late in the fall, the large boulders on the bottom were slippery and difficult to walk on. Leading the pack, Ranger and I ran into one major obstacle after another. Six-foot waterfalls with car-size boulders on either side made continuing straight up the creek channel impossible in some places.

When encountering these roadblocks, Ranger and I hiked up the steep bank of the creek and around the obstruction before working back down into the creek bed to continue moving upstream. Given the heavy tree and brush growth on either side of the creek, this meant climbing up a steep seventy-degree slope through a wall of branches and brush, which was, to be blunt, a pain in the ass. It was so steep in some places in fact, that we used our rifle slings as field-expedient climbing ropes to assist each other in making progress without falling into the rocky creek bottom 25 yards below. For the rest of the day, the team continued moving up the creek slowly, following Ranger's and my trial and error attempts to get around a major obstruction in the creek. By 6:00 p.m. we had been hiking for eleven hours and had descended and ascended 3,500 feet. Everyone on the team was tired and reaching his limit and we still had 500 feet straight uphill to go to get out of the creek channel and back to the trucks.

Within an hour, Ranger and I reached the top of the creek drainage and climbed out of the creek onto a grassy hillside. The grass field extended all the way to the top of the ridge where our trucks were parked, another 300 yards ahead. The best part of reaching the field was the lack of trees or brush anywhere between our vehicles and us. We had a straight, unobstructed shot at our command post, and we were elated. With the sun setting quickly at our backs and late afternoon shadows growing across the grass field, Ranger and I hustled as fast as possible to reach our trucks at the command post.

Relieved to be at the trucks, we met up with Jim, the ranch owner, and Mundst, the MET sergeant. After peeling our packs off and grabbing and guzzling some cold water and Gatorade, I gave the men a quick sit-rep. Like us, Jim and Mundst were disappointed we had not found an active grow site. Like the rest of us, however, they were intrigued we had found evidence of a grow somewhere below Day Mountain.

With the sun setting fast, Ranger and I wasted no time dwelling on this. We walked to the edge of the ranch to scan the grassy field below us, looking for any of our teammates to surface from the creek and pop out on the lower edge of the field. With the glare of the setting sun washing out the image in my pocket binoculars,

I could barely make out the first operator surfacing from the creek channel onto the field. It was Rails. And although he looked tired he was moving quickly. He stopped, smiled, and gave us the thumbs-up. Twenty yards behind him was Snake, moving steadily uphill and not taking his eyes off the field in front of him. Like the rest of the team, he just wanted to get to the trucks.

A few minutes later, a radio request from Rails had Ranger and me hiking back down the ridge across the field without our gear. Given the long and tough hike so far, some of our team members were fatigued and moving slowly. Slightly refreshed and feeling much lighter without packs, rifles, and extra ammunition, we made fast time down the ridge and started taking the packs and rifles from the rest of our team. A little lighter now, the whole team made better time to the trucks.

With everyone at the trucks, Snake conducted a quick debriefing of the day's events and conveyed his appreciation for everyone's hard work. The thirteen-hour recon was the toughest, steepest, and most difficult hike to date for our team, and everyone had done well.

After hydrating and snacking quickly with the team, I noticed Snake standing on the edge of the ranch fence line alone. I walked over to him. Snake was looking silently and intensely out across the vast Hondo drainage at the fiery red sunset over the south San Francisco Bay. With the instant temperature drop as the sun descended over the western hills, we both caught a chill as we continued to take in the amazing sunset in front of us. Neither of us wanted to break the peacefulness of such an amazing sight and did not speak for several minutes.

I did not have to ask what was on his mind. Snake's expression and the grin on his face said it all. We would be back sooner than later. And as tough as that day was, we were both eager for the next adventure.

❖

Before heavy rains started in late November we hiked two more drainages into the Arroyo Hondo. Starting from the Badger Ranch and a property to the north, each hike was similar to that first hike in October. Challenging, arduous, and steep, with only one drainage explored each day because of the time involved, the MET slowly eliminated possible grow site areas. On these recons, we made sure to explore every tributary that could possibly hold water to avoid missing anything. Overlooking any possibility of a grow site on these hikes could mean long-term failure, especially given how much more ground we needed to cover every time we did not find a garden.

On one hike, we found remnants of the last known cultivation site in the Arroyo Hondo. Eradicated in 2001, the grow was remote and huge. Almost 50,000 plants were taken out on that raid. The site was so elaborate and had been in operation for so long, the growers had actually built an adobe mud cooking stove in their kitchen area. Finding this old grow site was a bittersweet success for us. While we never want to see growers return to an old grow site, if we had found an active grow site in this spot again, our elusive search would be over. But this garden was just as it had been left that summer day when so may task force officers raided it. Relatively untouched from six years ago, the camp, kitchen, piles of supplies, and spider webs of numerous water lines were overgrown with heavy vegetation. Our team realized we had discovered a grow operation from long ago that could use some cleaning up at some point in the future.

The team found more remnants of cultivation activity in the other drainages we explored throughout November. We saw shards of black plastic sheeting for makeshift water catch basins and random pieces of black plastic pipe and other garden trash basins in the bottom of several drainages, but we never found an active grow site.

Frustrated and puzzled, and with heavy rains already beginning, we left the Hondo for the rest of the year. We knew we needed to rest up for the next season and reevaluate our approach to finding this elusive garden. We were running out of drainages to check, and we were coming up with nothing.

During the last hike of the month and on the final climb out of that steep drainage, Rails and I shared our thoughts. From the frustrated look on his face it was clear Rails was as disappointed as I was. Both of us realized, however, that the most difficult cases to solve took a lot of effort, persistence, and patience, and this kept us motivated to keep at it. Working special operations cases like this is the ultimate challenge for a game warden or other special operations enforcement officers because they are oftentimes difficult, exhausting, and time consuming. Both of us had been confident that we would have a cultivation site located by now, especially after so many recon hikes. As we crested the ridgeline and finished our climb to the truck, we shared one final concern. This grow was starting to haunt us. And every additional day spent looking for this elusive site just made the haunting even more extreme. Regardless, we were not giving up. Regardless of the challenge, finding this grow and catching these growers was going to be one of the best rewards of all our MET missions, and it would be a much sweeter reward when we finally found and shut down these guys. It was just a matter of time, and their day would come, hopefully sooner than later.

The start of a new season in April 2007 had the entire MET eager to get back in the woods and explore the Arroyo Hondo. Trying once again to find the mystery grow or at least eliminate another

A MET operator moves through a marijuana garden with M14 rifle. The tall, thick plants make visibility and movement through a grow site difficult and dangerous.

This grow site in Red Creek, on the Henry Coe State Park border, was spotted from the air and contained 16,000 pot plants.

MET tactical tracking operators short-hauling into the Bohlman Road crime scene under the CAMP helicopter shortly following the gunfight.

A grower's Smith and Wesson semi-automatic pistol from the Bodfish Creek Operation. Fortunately, he was caught before he was able to use it.

The skull of a mountain lion poached by growers in the Santa Cruz mountains. Many protected species are casualties in these illegal grow sites.

A typical grower's camp full of trash, pesticides, fertilizers, and other poisons found in an active cultivation site on Palassou Ridge in 2004.

Typically, marijuana gardens are cultivated as the understory for taller trees and bushes. The canopy of the native plants helps to hide them from detection from the air. Plants are fed by a timed drip irrigation system that delivers water, often enriched with fertilizer, to each plant.

Cheetah and the author with a trophy three-point blacktail buck poached by growers on the Palassou Ridge cultivation site.

The 129th Air Rescue Squadron's Pave Hawk helicopter lowers operators into the Sierra Azul site for the environmental clean-up operation.

Cheetah, Markos, and the author from the MET about to short-haul out of the Bohlman Road crime scene.

Marijuana growers stay with their gardens 24/7 for months at a time, living in camouflaged shelters like this one that are furnished with propane stoves, cots, stores of canned food, and radios. Some even have exercise equipment.

Cadet explorers, Boy Scouts, and MET operators remove trash and pollutants from the Mt. Hamilton eradication site.

Trash found on marijuana garden sites includes gardening equipment, clothing, pesticide sprayers, fertilizers, cooking utensils, sleeping bags, tarps, rat poison, plant cultivation materials, ammunition, and discarded food packages and cans.

A military Pave Hawk hoists a load of polluting trash out of the Hicks Road cultivation site during a clean-up operation.

drainage as a possible grow site, we completed another all-day hell hike down to the river's edge and back up. Again, we found nothing. At this point, the MET had explored all four primary drainages between Black Mountain and Day Mountain, with still no grow site.

By June we had eliminated the four primary canyons above the river as possibilities, and we shifted gears to keep searching for the garden. The team decided to navigate through and explore the Arroyo Hondo riverbed itself, which was always a goal of mine even before this operation began. In order to do so, we needed two days and an overnight stay in the river drainage to have the time necessary to cover the entire 18-mile stretch of the Hondo between its origin below Mount Hamilton and its end into Calaveras Reservoir so many miles downstream.

Snake, Mojo, Rails, Grit, and I made up the five-man recon team for the two-day adventure. Grit was the youngest and newest member of my Department of Fish and Game warden squad and was just starting his career. This hike was a perfect exploration at close range of the remotest and most inaccessible area of his patrol district, and he was excited to be part of the team.

Our mission was simple: Hike downstream along the river and check for evidence of cultivation and poaching activity along the way. We wanted to have plenty of time to explore *any* side channel or tributary into the river that looked promising. Given the steep areas of the river where car-size boulders and deep pools and waterfalls made traveling along the riverbed impossible in some places, we all knew the hike was going to be brutally *slow*. Coupling this with 100-plus-degree heat, we all knew staying focused and alert was critical to being injury-free and successful over the next two days. If any team member broke a leg, twisted an ankle, suffered a rattlesnake bite, or had any other injury this far into the backcountry, the whole team would be compromised and our mission would be over. With the difficult terrain and the possibility of hike-ending injuries, our team would have to be extra careful on this adventure.

To reach the headwaters of the Arroyo Hondo, we dropped down a steep ridgeline above the river. Starting just across the canyon and not far from the peak of Mount Hamilton, the view of the Lick Observatory telescopes and science buildings was impressive before we descended and entered the riverbed below. After descending almost 2,000 feet and finally reaching the slow-moving river, we all noticed the same thing. The solitude and peacefulness of this waterway was unmatched and seemed remoter than any place I could think of in our patrol districts. The lack of any trash, debris, or other signs of human presence just added to the purity of this place. Once assembled along the water's edge we started our hike downstream. Hiking at times along both banks of the river, we hopped boulder to boulder within the water's flow, moving steadily downstream.

For the first 6 miles we saw a mix of wildlife and fish species in the river's pools but only one sign of human presence. Mojo and Grit noticed a small fire ring made up of softball-size river rocks lying discreetly on a sand beach along the water's edge. Given the fresh ash in the ring, it was evident this fire pit had been used recently. On each side of the pit were two man-size depressions in the sand, showing us where two people had slept for the night around the fire. With the rest of the beach devoid of any human signs, we realized this had most likely been a temporary camp, probably used for the night while someone was passing through the area. Perhaps it was a growers' recon camp used while they were accessing a water source or looking for a supply route. More likely, though, it was a poacher's camp for people taking trout and other wildlife species illegally. Either way our team was surprised to see this remote campsite so far into the backcountry. We were all reminded that it was possible we were not alone on the river, and that others who may have been up to no good had been on this beach recently.

We continued hiking down the river through the afternoon, exploring every side canyon and possible water source tributary that could support a grow site. Late in the day at about mile 12, I was on point and guiding our team slowly along a narrow sandy beach. Just right of my shoulder was a rock canyon wall, while just a few feet left of my feet was the river. At this place the river formed a large pool spanning about 10 feet across and 3 feet in depth.

As I continued hiking along the canyon wall, a familiar smell caught my attention. Somewhere above or ahead of our position, it smelled like someone was using a propane cookstove. This smell was familiar to all of us. Since growers are often cooking with portable propane stoves when our team makes contact on an eradication mission, this smell was disturbing to us all. I looked back at Snake, number two in our line, and pointed to my nose. He nodded his head in agreement indicating he knew and recognized the smell as well. I drew my Glock pistol from my holster and held it at the low ready position ahead of me, scanning for anything dangerous ahead as we continued to walk downriver.

As I continued to scan for threats a surprising and completely unusual sight caught my eye. Across the river pool on our left was another narrow sandy beach with a large cottonwood tree on the upstream edge of the sandbar. The low-hanging branches of the tree almost reached the sand on the beach providing the only shade on that side of the river in the late afternoon sun. My first thought was what a great campsite that beach would make for the night when suddenly it registered what else I was seeing. Three mountain lions, all lying in the shade and on the edge of the water under the cottonwood, were sound asleep on the cool, shaded sand. Two of the great cats actually had their paws in the water, clearly doing everything possible to cool down on that 100-degree day.

It's extremely rare to see even a single mountain lion in the wild, let alone three. Since we had moved quietly downriver making little noise and were walking into the hot breeze, this lion family had not heard or smelled us yet. And since they were dozing, none of them had seen any of us yet either. Seeing three 100-pound lions this close was surreal and a career highlight for all of us. Given the keen senses and awareness of mountain lions and their solitary nature when full grown, what we were witnessing was simply not supposed to happen. Again, the remoteness of the Hondo caught me, and I realized these cats had probably *never* seen a human before. The Arroyo Hondo was their home, and we were intruding in their bedroom.

After the initial excitement of seeing these creatures passed, our team's safety came to mind. What would happen when they woke up? Knowing that mountain lions are very wary of people in general and that contrary to myths and panic-based fears, they *seldom* attack humans, I still had concerns given the situation. Snake and I were less than 15 yards from the trio now with a rock wall behind us and nowhere to go but right past them or back upriver. We were a bit stuck at the moment, and the thought of waking and startling the lions while this close to them with no escape route was not a pleasant one.

As I covered the sleeping trio with my pistol, Snake moved up slowly behind me to cover the three cats with his AR15. I glanced quickly at Snake and noticed the grin on his face. He too was amazed and pleased to see these large predators snoozing away. With Snake now shoulder to shoulder with me covering the lions, I looked behind me and saw Grit climbing over the last set of boulders 20 yards behind us before landing on the sandy beach. As soon as he looked up in our direction, I pointed at the cats across the river to make sure he saw them. Grit froze in his tracks when he saw the cats. Reacting just like we did, Grit's eyes widened when he realized how close the three lions were, and they remained motionless as he drew his Glock pistol. Staying still, Grit covered the cats from his position as the rest of the team continued to advance to our location.

The mature male lion in the group was the largest of the three cats and was starting to stir. Realizing we were not going to remain unseen for long, we prepared for the worst and hoped the lions would simply spook and run downstream and away from us. Just as Mojo was climbing over the boulder stack, the big male woke up and looked right at us. Shocked to see us so close to his pride, the dominant cat jumped up and instinctively crouched toward us in an attack posture. Ready to engage and open fire if the big cat attacked, but praying not to have to, we continued to cover the surprised lion and held our ground with nowhere to go. Our standoff lasted only a few seconds as the male hissed and growled before the other two females woke up. With all three cats up and aware of our presence, the pride jumped up and wasted no time bolting downstream. Within seconds, all three cats were out of sight, with only the fading echoes of their growls and screams off the surrounding steep canyon walls left behind.

Still holding our weapons at the ready, Mojo, Grit, Snake, and I let out sighs of relief that the lions had left the area without confrontation. As we slowly lowered and holstered our guns, Rails jumped over the boulder stack to join us on the beach. Realizing he had not seen the cats before they fled, we all gave him an excited update about what had just happened. Rails was amazed by our story but also disappointed to have missed all the excitement. Point men have all the fun! Hopefully, the bolting lions would not alert any growers downstream that our team was near. Given the rare and lucky encounter with the three lions, however, we thought the trade off was well worth it.

Our team waited for a few minutes to make sure the lion trio was well downstream before continuing our hike. It was the end of the day, and we had been hiking for almost ten hours straight. Given the heat and fatigue setting in for everyone, we decided to stop for the night. With no other camping spots to use in that area, we backtracked to the beach where the lions had been napping. We named it Lion Beach and settled there for the night. Mojo, Grit, and I set up our bed rolls under the cottonwood tree right where the lions had been sleeping, while Snake and Rails settled on the narrow beach just downstream from the tree.

As we set camp, we noticed a narrow opening in the rock canyon wall above the beach. We discovered it was a lion den and contained numerous skeletons of small mammals and rodents. This beach was not just a spot these cats had found to cool down during a hot day. It was their home, and we were going to borrow it for the night.

We all had an eerie feeling that night, and our anxiety level was elevated knowing we were sleeping in a lions' den. Not to mention that the propane we smelled earlier that day indicated growers were somewhere in the area. Even so, we all appreciated the beauty of the canyon and the soothing sound of the river so close to our camp that night, and we managed to get a little sleep between perimeter security duties.

With a much shorter distance to cover to reach our pickup spot the following day, we made good time to our extraction point. But we still had not found a grow site. Fortunately, though, we had eliminated any possibilities within or close to the riverbed itself. We also realized a grow site was likely above us given the cooking stove smell we all detected just before we got to Lion Beach. And we had seen three mountain lions. Not a bad couple of days' work. Like past recons into the Hondo, we all knew we needed to keep looking and would check the few remaining canyons still untouched by our team. Through process of elimination we were getting closer to finally finding the elusive grow operation. With arrest and eradication missions on known gardens starting shortly though, we knew our scouting time into the Hondo would have to be postponed until the following spring.

When our operations in the Hondo started up again in April 2008, the MET finally got a break. Another trail camera photo from the Badger Ranch above the Arroyo Hondo showed two more growers laden with backpacks and handheld cultivation supplies hiking toward the river. Because this picture was taken from another camera on another road on the ranch, we now had a more precise idea of the location the growers were likely using for their operation. The photos were taken almost a year and a half apart, but when examined together, they told us so much. We were able to triangulate the growers' approach and get a solid starting point on finding out where they had to be operating.

In May 2008 the MET conducted one more overnight recon into the Hondo, this time cutting the distance of our hike by a third. This time the team was made up of Snake, Rails, Markos, and me. We chose to access the river by descending into one of the last unexplored drainages near Black Mountain above the river. This would eliminate another canyon in the area where the photos were taken, in addition to seeing if anything cultivation related had developed in the river itself since our overnight recon thirteen months ago. The hike yielded more cultivation debris signs in the river drainage itself but, again, no active grow site. Still frustrated but narrowing the location possibilities even more, we now knew where the grow site had to be located within a half-mile area. We were getting very close to finding our objective, and excitement was building within the MET.

Now it was time to go up in the air and find this grow. In mid-July 2008 Obe, a part-time MET member and marijuana spotter flying the Santa Clara County sheriff's office helicopter, *Star One*, hit pay dirt and made the best aerial find in our team's four-year history. Obe's nickname is "Eagle Eyes" and for good reason. No one comes close to being able to find well-hidden and remotely located dope grows like Obe. Although *very* well hidden, the grow north-west of Day Mountain was found by Obe just where it was suspected to be. After almost two years and many hours and days and nights of recon hikes in the woods, we had finally found the mystery grow! And as an added bonus, we found it right in the middle of growing season before prime harvest time. Perfect timing!

Within just days of Obe's find, Rails conducted a quick pre-eradication scout to confirm the grow from the ground. Rails not only found the grow but also a quiet trail into the grow site from the high ground. It was perfect for stalking and getting light running teams up to chase down and catch some growers.

In late August 2008 we were ready to eradicate the Day Moun-tain garden. Because of the remote location and the steep terrain that predominated the grow, we knew we could not complete this mission effectively without helicopter support. Even though this was a Santa Clara County MET operation, we requested the help of CAMP's Region 3 team to assist with the mission. CAMP was available to help that day, and we were grateful. Not only could we use CAMP's bird to haul out loads of marijuana, but we also had the added asset of several CAMP operators to assist in eradicating plants. And with CAMP involved, those of us on the MET had an added treat. We would be short-hauled out of the garden by CAMP's helicopter and would not have to hike out of the grow at the end of the day. After a long day of chasing bad guys, eradicating dope, and repairing environmental damage, a short-haul ride out of a grow site versus hiking straight uphill to get to a command post is a blessing.

We established the operations command post on a large grass meadow inside Badger Ranch. This allowed us to park our trucks close to the jump-off starting point for our hike into the grow site. This meadow was also large enough to be an ideal landing zone for the CAMP team and its helicopter. Like other operations, the MET would stalk into the grow first to arrest growers and secure the entire grow site. Following this, the CAMP team's supervisor would start dropping operators into the garden two at a time for the eradication phase of the operation.

Rails was the case agent, meaning he would be overseeing this operation for the day, so he conducted the briefing for the entire team. We would be running a larger single team that day with light runners up front with our point men. With Cheetah working out of the area at the time, my running partner for the day was Spag. While not usually a runner, Spag was in good shape, fast, and would never give up on any chase. As we assembled for the briefing we smiled as we shook hands, eager as always to work together on an operation. Spag had so many training duties that precluded him from going on many of our missions that his joining us that day was a treat, especially given the fact that this was the Arroyo Hondo mystery grow site that had taken us so much time and effort to find.

Rails gave a brief synopsis of the time and work that had gone into finding the grow site and the especially dangerous nature of this one. Given how sophisticated and remote we all knew this grow to be, we expected to encounter guns and men ready to use them.

And given the quiet stalkable trail going into the grow, getting close enough for a chase and arrest was probable.

As Rails reviewed our team list and stack formation for the day, I was pleased to know that Snake and Apache would be up front on point, since they were always a good combination. Following them were Spag and me in light gear and ready to run, followed by Rails and Hoff. Hoff is another skilled operator who works on the team part-time, and he and Rails were backing us up with two more AR15 rifles. A K-9 handler and member of SERT, Hoff was prepared and ready for a good day's work in the woods.

In the tail gun position was Doc, our special ops medic. As with other eradication operations where we expected excessive resistance or violence, Doc was there to provide medical support in the unfortunate event one of us got hurt. Not only great at providing field trauma aid, Doc was a hard worker when it came to eradicating plants and restoring impacted waterways in a grow site.

Woody, the final member of our team, was our operations supervisor for the day. Staying at the command post to coordinate with the CAMP team when it arrived later that morning, Woody was bummed about not going into the woods with us. However, he had an important role: Get the helicopter team staged and operational quickly and efficiently.

With a final weapons and equipment check completed, Snake guided our team west and over the edge of the hillside into the canyon below Day Mountain. The trail descended quickly, and in just a few minutes our team was assembled under the shady canopy of some oak trees. Under these oaks, the trail was well worn, and at least three sets of fresh boot prints were evident on the ground. All three sets were headed into the grow in front of us. We all realized that we had to be wary of at least three men.

As we descended farther into the canyon on the growers' trail, the oak and bay tree terrain changed to brushy chemise and coyote brush—ideal and common terrain for growing dope. Slowly moving through the brushy trail, Snake and Apache held up their left hands in fists, stopping the team instantly. Both point men had seen the start of a marijuana garden 20 yards ahead of us. I looked ahead to see that the plants were tall, about 5 to 6 feet in height, and topped with ripe buds about a foot in length. These plants were ready for harvest, and fortunately we had not missed this phase of the cultivation process.

After assessing the garden and detecting no movement, Snake and Apache resumed a slow stalk farther down the trail into the grow site. When we reached the first group of plants, we were all impressed with the elaborate and camouflaged watering system. All the black plastic water lines were painted a dull green and brown. Made to blend perfectly with the surrounding terrain, these irrigation hoses could not be seen from the air. Also impressive was the placement of all the budded plants in the brush and the small-tree canopy above. The plants were strategically interspersed throughout the brush in random order, almost impossible to see until we were a few feet from them. This attention to detail did not surprise any of us given everything we had learned about this operation in the last two seasons we had been working it.

We were moving slowly through the brush when the grow opened up into a larger garden about 25 yards square. This garden was larger than the previous one, better concealed, and more elaborate with its irrigation system. Like the first plants we had seen on our stalk, these were all tall and ready for harvest as well. The trail continued along the northern edge of the garden with mature plants to our left and a shale wall to our right. With only a 2-foot-wide trail to maneuver with packs, weapons, and other gear, we were all moving slowly and carefully to avoid detection.

The plants below us had been recently watered, indicating grow-ers were close. Snake slowed the team down even more as we inched forward on the narrow trail.

All four of us noticed sudden movement 30 yards ahead and froze in our tracks. Tall plants ahead moving side to side indicated a person was walking through the grow in our direction. With nowhere good to hide, the team moved into what little concealment we could find on the narrow trail and jumped into the first row of marijuana plants to our left. Half on and half off the trail, and with our weapons pointed at the approaching man, all we could do was just wait and be ready for anything. Spag and I peeled off our packs, and with our handguns at the low ready, prepared for a sprint just seconds away.

Seconds later, we got a look at the man walking in our direction: a young Hispanic in his midtwenties, wearing brown jeans and a light brown jacket. He was less than 20 yards ahead of us now and headed right for us on the same trail. When the grower suddenly stopped and looked in our direction, we knew he had detected something. The grower seemed to know we were ahead and just stared for the next few seconds. Being intimately familiar with this site, the felon was quickly realizing that whatever was mixed into that first row of marijuana plants did not belong there.

Hoping it was a fellow grower, the man asked, "Primo?" When he did not get a response, he asked again. After an uncomfortable pause of a few seconds, Apache took the initiative and replied, "Si, amigo" trying to comfort the man and keep him from turning and sprinting away from the team. With the trail so narrow and the rock wall blocking our mobility, Spag and I were stuck behind Apache and Snake and could not start our chase. We wanted to yell with frustration, but we had no choice except to stay still until our point men could get out of the way.

While it was a clever effort on Apache's part, the grower was not buying our ruse. The smile on his face changed to a look of shock as he put it all together and realized there were armed men in camouflage staring back at him. Before his expression changed again, the man turned and sprinted quickly back through the grow.

Without hesitation, Spag and I jumped up and pushed past Apache and Snake to start chasing this grower, already building momentum with his head start. Spag was on point and picking up speed, with me tailing less than a yard behind while the distance to the fleeing felon was now 30 yards.

Once past our point guys and free to sprint, Spag and I made good time. We could see the grower ahead still moving quickly past the last of the marijuana plants in the grow site. Seconds later, we too cleared the last of the plants, and Spag and I now found ourselves on an open grass slope with the rocky trail curving ahead of us to the north. The rock canyon wall continued on the right of us and had a more gradual pitch to it. While not quite as steep, it still left us little room to maneuver on our right side.

The grower was fast, really fast, and navigated smoothly over the rocky trail maintaining his pace. I wish I could say the same for us, but the unfamiliar terrain and numerous loose rock and potholes in the trail were making things very difficult. Just as we were starting to gain on the fleeing felon, my right foot slipped on a loose boulder, and I collapsed onto my right shin as my leg bent and hit another large rock on the trail. Without hesitation I used the momentum of the fall to roll over my slammed shin and recovered on my feet to resume the chase. I was only five yards behind Spag now and caught up to him in the next few seconds.

Up ahead we could see the man pulling something metallic and shiny from his waistband as he continued to run. Realizing it was a pistol, our tension increased again as we continued to cover the grower with our handguns. As if knowing that pulling a pistol on us meant certain suicide, the grower suddenly threw it down in the brush along the trail and continued his dash to escape. The good news for all of us involved was that he did not wish to start a gunfight.

The grower was only 20 yards ahead of us now and appeared to be slowing down slightly, a good thing given the throbbing ache in my right shin. We had been chasing this man for about 80 yards at this point and still had the speed to continue and close the gap for a catch when suddenly I lost Spag.

As if stepping on an open trapdoor and being eaten up by the trail itself, Spag dropped out of sight below the trail and disappeared. Still running as fast as I could, I glanced down as I passed the spot where Spag had vanished. A rockslide chute where the trail should have been was on the ground below and this was clearly what Spag had slipped into. Like a semicircular dirt water slide, the chute dropped to another marijuana garden about 20 yards below our position on the trail. I slowed down and looked back for just a second to see Spag standing up from his slide among several tall marijuana plants. He waved up at the rest of the team behind us that he was okay, and I turned and continued my pursuit.

My right shin throbbed as I ran down the rocky trail, slowly closing the distance to the fleeing gunman ahead. Now passing many rows of budding marijuana plants in yet another grow, the chase continued to traverse the rocky trail. The felon was only 20 yards ahead of me as I tried to gain on his stride.

I was not about to lose this guy and give up three frustrating seasons of hard work trying to find this grow. Anything less would be unacceptable. I could see a dark canyon and creek bed up ahead. And the bend along the hillside indicated one thing; unexplored land deep in the heart of the grower's operation with no one to cover me. And worse yet, these terrain changes made for a perfect ambush site.

Growing more anxious as we closed the distance to the creek, I realized 40 more yards and my chase was over, one way or another. Not willing to risk suicide, I would not cross that creek and chase him alone out of view of my team members. I had some comfort knowing Snake and Apache were running behind and covering me as best they could. But with heavy packs and AR15 rifles holding them back, the gap between us had widened to almost 50 yards.

Delayed for only a split second when the grower reached the creek, the felon made a quick jump across it and resumed his frantic sprint. Within seconds he was out of view around a bend in the trail above the creek channel. Seconds later I reached the creek in full stride, jumped across it, and stopped for a second to look back for my closest support. Snake and Apache were now out of view back around a bend in the trail as our gap widened to about 80 yards now.

Panting heavily and gasping for air, I looked back up at the trail ahead and realized the chase was over. I had the urge to sprint up the bank of the creek and continue the pursuit but decided against it. This was the point of no return, and I had to give up and accept it. This one was going to get away. I stopped running immediately forcing my body to a halt and threw both of my arms into the air venting my extreme frustration. Some days it just does not work out in our favor, and this chase was an example of one of those days.

A few seconds later Snake and Apache caught up to me and I gave a quick sit-rep on what I had seen before the grower disappeared. Immediately following the update, I jogged back on the trail to find the brush line where the grower had thrown the pistol. Within a minute I could see the grip of the handgun sticking up in the brush within a foot of the edge of the trail. I removed the pistol from the brush and noticed it was a Ruger Mark II stainless steel .22

caliber semiautomatic target pistol. After removing the magazine from the pistol and clearing the loaded chamber of a live cartridge, I locked the bolt at the rear of the gun's receiver and showed it to Snake. The magazine and chamber were full of high-velocity hollow point rounds, and while dirty and poorly maintained, the gun was functional. I was relieved the gunman had chosen to throw the pistol down as opposed to using it against us.

After securing the pistol as evidence, Snake and I backtracked a little farther on the trail to find Spag. Looking down below the trail we could see Spag and Rails on the eastern edge of the garden. A radio check revealed the rest of the team had cleared the bottom garden Spag had slid into and they were all waiting our return.

When we climbed down the slope to join the team, Spag and I discussed the botched chase. He was bummed about sliding down the chute and leaving me to run solo when we were so close to catching the grower. I felt the same about chasing the grower alone without him. Regardless, we were happy to be in one of the many large gardens in the Day Mountain operation and felt content knowing none of this dope would make it to the street or yield even a penny on the black market, especially since this grow was worth at least 45 million dollars.

For the next two hours, we explored every trail, watering system, camp, kitchen, and marijuana processing area throughout the operation. As suspected, this operation was large and had been in place for at least the past three years if not longer. And given the number of sleeping bags in camp and the number of gardens spread out along the hillside, we knew we had missed several more suspects that day.

As soon as we had finished checking all the gardens and trails for suspects, the CAMP team started dropping into the gardens around us from the helicopter. Two operators at a time were lowered into the grow sites, and once on the ground the team wasted no time in chopping down and eradicating plants.

Once the eradication teams were all in place and removing plants, I hiked down to check the campsite and the environmental crime damage along the waterways. For the next two hours a handful of us on the MET removed water impoundments and other pollutants from the two flowing tributaries. We also located and identified all the trash-filled sites throughout the gardens that would need attention later during the cleanup season. By the day's end, the MET and CAMP had eradicated and short-hauled out of the woods by helicopter about 15,000 plants, all of which were ready or nearly ready to be harvested. Not a bad haul for such a remote grow in the Arroyo Hondo backcountry. This grow was one of the larger ones eradicated by our MET during the 2008 season. Even more significant and important was the fact that this garden operation had gone undiscovered with successful harvests for many years before today, making today's mission even more rewarding.

With the day approaching five o'clock and both teams exhausted, the CAMP chopper returned from removing the last load of pot to start short-hauling us out of the woods and back to the command post. I was paired up with Apache, and we were about to experience the longest, most scenic, and exhilarating short-haul ride of our careers thus far.

With the distance limit for operator safety on a short-haul flight being 5 miles, today's ride was going to test that distance. After putting on and securing our short-haul harnesses and helmets, Apache and I conducted a buddy check by making sure all of our belts and fasteners were tightly secured.

Once the check was completed, we walked out onto the edge of a large granite cliff on the side of the steep hillside overlooking the Arroyo Hondo River below. On the top edge of the rocky cliff next to the hillside was a plateau just wide enough for me and Apache to stand on and wait for the chopper to return and take us to the command post.

As we waited I looked over the edge of the cliff and saw the tiny river snaking below us in the canyon 1,300 feet below our position. The drop was almost straight down for several hundred feet from the cliff's edge, and a dizzying wave of vertigo hit me for a second. Being lifted off this cliff for our short-haul ride was going to be awesome as neither one of us had ever been extracted from such a steep spot before. Even though we had short-hauled numerous times over the past three seasons, the excitement of today's ride was generating another adrenaline rush, and I felt a little shaky as a result.

A few minutes later the helicopter was hovering above us. When we gave the hand signal to descend, the pilot slowly lowered the short-haul cable into our hands with pinpoint precision. As soon as we grabbed the cable, we connected the two cable extensions to our harnesses and were ready to start our journey. We gave the hand signal for the pilot to head out, and the wild ride was under way.

Right after the chopper lifted us a few feet off the rock, the unexpected occurred, and we were suddenly free-falling with the chopper at a fast rate a few hundred feet into the river basin below. Like a roller-coaster drop of thirteen stories or more, the fast descent off the cliff and into the river basin below was an exhilarating rush. After about a 300-foot drop, and just in time to settle our stomachs, the chopper leveled its altitude, and we were flying southeast at a constant 100 mph. Apache looked at me as we held on to our harness cables tightly and just smiled. While the ride was exhilarating, the view was even more breathtaking. Feeling like eagles flying above the Arroyo Hondo, we could see the river for miles as we followed it upstream from so far above. Having hiked and camped in that stretch of river just a few months ago, it was an added treat to be seeing it from 1,000 feet above at such a high rate of speed.

The ride seemed to last forever as we raced across the sky following the river below. This was the end of an eradication operation that took almost two and a half years of hard work and challenges to complete. And it was fitting to be seeing the vast and remote area we had spent so many hours hiking and exploring over those tough years from a long line under the CAMP bird. The view from that high put everything in perspective. I suddenly realized why it had taken us so long to find this grow. It was located in the largest, steepest, most wooded and remotest mountain range in the county. As we passed just below the peak of Day Mountain and continued on to the landing zone, I smiled with elation and relief in finally finding the grow that haunted our team for so long, and that no one got hurt in the process. When I looked at Apache again, I noticed the same smile. Those grins remained all the way home as Apache and I savored the rest of the ride to the command post. Rewarded and visually reminded of the wildlife resources in the Arroyo Hondo we had done much to protect by running this criminal crew out of the woods today, we savored our afternoon success at the end of a very long operation well done.

CHAPTER 6

Fay Creek Operation: Fish and Game Teams Take the Lead

Trust your men and they will be true to you; treat them greatly,
and they will show themselves great.

—RALPH WALDO EMERSON

A fellow lieutenant named Nate called me in the early summer of 2008. He was a cadet when I first met him ten years ago when I was teaching at the California Department of Fish and Game Resource Academy, but now he was a tactically oriented, driven, and professional game warden. It seemed that in his district, which includes Kern County and is southeast of Santa Clara County and in the Central Valley, the Department of Fish and Game was developing a MET similar to the one I was involved in. Being the first marijuana eradication team in the state to include and prefer game wardens as members, the equipment, training, and lessons learned by our team in Santa Clara County could help Nate's team get started effectively.

Since our MET had been active since 2005, we had some trial and error operational and equipment lessons to pass on to the Kern County team that could save time, money, and maybe lives. Knowing that Nate's team was still developing and that its members were some highly motivated game wardens I'd helped train in the past made it even better.

I heard the excitement in Nate's voice as we shared stories about our teams and future operations. With his assistant chief's complete support of the department's objectives in the environmental aspect of marijuana eradication, Nate was allowed to outfit his operators right from the start. Camouflage BDUs ideally suited for his team's operating environment, backpacks, radio equipment, short-haul rescue harnesses, helmets, and other tactical essentials were issued to the team at startup. This let Nate's men not only run operations more efficiently and safely but also show allied agency task force members the professionalism and skill sets of game wardens in general. It's not just the general public that has little knowledge of what game wardens do; it's also other law enforcement agencies that know little or nothing about our roles.

Having received similar support from the Department of Fish and Game's Chief of Patrol Nancy Foley and my Assistant Chief Carmela during our team's development a few years ago, I could relate to Nate's excitement. That kind of support from command staff members above our pay grades made all the difference in the world and significantly increased our team members' motivation. Like me, Nate was not assigned to form a team and get involved in arrest and eradication missions, but did so out of a desire to be progressive with his game wardens. He wanted to make a real difference in fighting the environmental crime caused by cultivation operations throughout his district, and continue to develop the important role California game wardens play in this area of rural special operations.

After going over equipment logistics and training details, Nate let the cat out of the bag. His team was working a grow site located on Fish and Game property in his district, and our department was taking the lead on it. The two groups were handling all the cultivation site surveillance, as well as tracking suspects to their homes; grow site monitoring and intelligence gathering; and coordinating, planning, and leading the arrest and eradication operation when the time was right. For the first time, this operation was one Fish and Game would be *leading* rather than *assisting*. This was a precedent-setting marijuana eradication operation with personnel from three other agencies—U.S. Forest Service and two county sheriff departments—working under our leadership. This was a first and quite an honor.

My excitement increased again when Nate broke down the details of the operation. Earlier in the year law enforcement personnel from his district had discovered growers working on the edge of the Canebrake Ecological Reserve, which is owned by the California Department of Fish and Game, located between Kern and Tulare Counties. Situated in the northeast corner of Kern County where the high desert meets the Sierras, this refuge is an extraordinary center of biodiversity. Five of the state's six bioregions are in this 1,400-acre refuge that is home to over 330 species of birds, 115 species of animals, and 2,000 species of plants. This is desert country, but Fay Creek, a north-south year-round flowing stream in Canebrake drains into the South Fork Valley, which is north of the south fork of the Kern River northeast of Lake Isabella. Because the stream flows year-round, it makes growing everything possible, including marijuana.

When investigating the site, the local law enforcement staff had discovered two marijuana cultivation areas along Fay Creek a few miles into the reserve. In addition, concentrated long-term surveillance had identified two growers, likely armed, working the cultivation site since earlier that spring. And the best part was yet to come. Nate went on to describe how his team had established the nexus between the grow site, other felons involved in the criminal conspiracy, their vehicles, and the residences where the processing and distribution of the high-dollar crop throughout the state and beyond was taking place. Because this operation was targeting not only those working within the garden sites but also those trafficking, selling, and processing the cash crop, we were looking for numerous co-conspirators to apprehend and prosecute.

I was thoroughly pumped up now. Before I could even say what was on my mind, Nate was already a step ahead. He suggested I come down with my team to help out during the arrest and eradication phase of the operation.

This operation hit close to home for us game wardens. Fay Creek is a pristine and sensitive waterway critical to the trout fishery in the creek and downstream into the Kern River, as well as being the life force that drives the explosion of biodiversity in Canebrake. It was critical that we stop and rectify the certain destruction to the creek as a result of this grow. And, as an operation led by the Department of Fish and Game, we were hoping to make history.

Before ending our phone call, we went over feasible times for the "takedown" to occur. A takedown is a coordinated operation where a number of wardens from around the state are brought together for an arrest. Mid-July was looking good for both of us. With that, we wished each other good luck and got off the phone, eager to meet soon and get this mission completed.

The Fay Creek mission was set for the third week of July. This was good timing as the first two weeks of the month were busy ones for our MET. The back-to-back Montebello Road foot chase and the Bohlman Road shooting incident had just happened. After just a short break, Nate called and invited me down to his district to meet with several of his team members as well as with operators on his county's allied agency MET to prepare for our upcoming operation. I was curious to see how groups in another part of the state were doing business. I wondered if they were arrest- and prosecution-oriented like our team, and I also wondered if our light running teams were similar.

When July 2008 arrived, I met with Nate and his team members Will, Connell, Rob, and Terry. Will and Connell were two of the few Fish and Game wardens assigned to CAMP teams for the summer, so they definitely knew their way around a dope garden. Terry and Rob had spent some time as well assisting their local task force on arrest and eradication operations over the past few years and were now working one of their own on the home front. After catching up for a minute, we walked into the office and settled in a small conference room to meet the other task force members and discuss the plan for the upcoming takedown just a few days away.

I was immediately impressed with the task force sergeant and two of his deputies assigned to the MET. They were not only SWAT team members for the Kern and Tulare County Sheriff's Departments and heavily involved in special operations in their respective agencies, but they all looked fit and ready to roll in the woods. As we talked before getting into the specifics of the operation, I learned these guys operated much like our team and focused on catching bad guys and not just eradicating plants.

The group's shared excitement was infectious as members described their season so far and how many growers they had caught by stalking and chasing them down. This team was also one of the few that was using light runners to get some arrests. When I found this out, the conversation ignited like wildfire, and war stories quickly filled the air. These guys could have filled in for anyone on my team back at home and vice versa. It's always a relief when operators from different teams think alike and get along so easily. This mission was getting to be more fun by the minute.

The mission planning went smoothly. Nate, as always, had prepared well for the upcoming takedown as he explained the history of the operation and the logistics of the mission. He had established a good command post, support staff, and the coordination that was needed between four teams on raid day. The entire plan was to have two arrest and eradication teams in the woods simultaneously to handle the grow, and two search and arrest warrant teams in the valley's cities to hit the suspects' homes first thing in the morning.

Nate and I agreed that two teams of about eight operators each would be ideal for the arrest mission in the grow. When Nate gave me the lists of operators from Fish and Game and the allied agency task force I knew we were in good shape. I would need to borrow Cheetah and Markos from northern California to assist on my team and round out the point and running positions for the mission. Getting to handpick our team members was a blessing. Now between Nate's squad, some superb task force officers, and my core MET operators, we had a solid team that could handle anything we encountered in the woods. And because this was the first arrest and eradication mission led by the Department of Fish and Game and was receiving a lot of attention from headquarters and the department's directorate, Nate and I wanted it done thoroughly and with the right people.

I would be leading the first arrest team into the grow site, while Connell from Nate's squad would lead the second team. I also had the advantage of having José, a SWAT officer and excellent runner on the task force, on my team who had run down and captured several growers in the past. Pairing him with Cheetah as the running team in the stack was an obvious move.

I knew I wanted some savvy operators up front on point, and Markos was a great choice. Also assigned to my team was Adam, a highly regarded law enforcement officer with the U.S. Forest Service and a member of the area task force. Adam's skill in tracking and finding grow sites and catching growers on and off national forests is legendary, and I could not think of a better pairing than Markos on point with him. In addition I had Pat, another game warden on my team who also had experience with videography, and several task force officers skilled in stalking and catching growers on the run. Pat would follow our team's progress and get video footage of the takedown for training and education purposes. In addition, Pat was a good runner, and could drop his camera and chase growers if necessary.

Connell was Nate's second team leader and his group of operators was looking good as well. Will, Rob, Tony, and John (the assistant chief of their district) from Fish and Game and several skilled task force members made up a good group.

After we looked at the team lists and broke down individual assignments, Nate turned our attention to a topographical map of the ecological reserve and the grow site itself. The terrain and gradual elevation changes provided ideal stalking conditions for both teams with plenty of cover to keep us out of view as we worked toward the growers. But as Nate talked, a caution light went on.

Seeing a great approach route on the map from the north, I asked Nate about the noise level on the ground. This was the middle of the dry season. Specifically, I wanted to know if there were trails on the property or wooded terrain approaches that we could navigate across and stalk quietly to get close enough to the growers without being detected. There's nothing like having two full-size teams noisily crunching leaves, grass, and branches to ruin a great operation. Given the likelihood of the growers being armed, I did not want our teams to be easy targets for ambush gunmen lying in wait.

When Nate looked up I could see he was troubled. He told us all that this late in the summer everything in the reserve would be dry, brittle, and difficult to traverse without making noise. Nate said, "Unfortunately it's going to be really tough for your team to sneak up on these guys. The ground conditions are just not that good for a stalk like you and your guys like to do. You will know what I mean when you see the terrain. It will be challenging to say the least."

I paused a minute and grinned. "Well Nate, like you, we never go after the easy ones and it would not be as rewarding to catch these guys if it was going to be easy. We may have to start extremely early, or hike twice as far, but if these guys are there tomorrow, we will find and catch them even if it takes us all morning."

Nate smiled at my confidence in our team's success, but the worried look on his face mirrored both of our thoughts. Until we had two growers safely in handcuffs, Nate and I were both aware there were no absolutes. Both of us realized we needed to not only do our jobs well, but also to get a little lucky in the process. And while Nate added there should be some game trails in the property, they would be few and far between.

Despite all this, I was still committed. I figured if our teams moved carefully and the growers were distracted tending their high-dollar plants, and the noise from Fay Creek covered up some of our movement, we might get lucky.

Looking again at the map, we established good approaches for both teams. My group would hike north away from the grow site from the eastern border road where the growers had been spotted so many months before. This would allow us to gain plenty of distance from the growers to mask our noise as we moved into position from the north well above the garden and any camp in the reserve.

Conversely, Connell's team had a good approach close to my team's starting point but would move west on a more direct route to the garden itself. While moving slowly, his guys would be able to get close enough to clearly see the garden and any growers working in it before being detected themselves. And as an added benefit, if they were detected, and bounced the growers out of the site, the felons would be headed in the direction of my team and would run right into us. This made for a perfect choke point to catch these guys should Connell's team spot them first.

This all looked good on paper, but as always with these operations, Murphy's Law usually kicks in and things seldom go as planned. And highly coordinated missions like this with multiple teams are even more likely to not go as planned. It's always a little nerve-racking to realize this, but it's also what adds excitement to the stew.

After the meeting I exchanged contact numbers with the task force officers and visited a bit longer with my Fish and Game buddies. We were bonding quickly for the upcoming operation, and considering we were from two different parts of the state and working together for the first time, it was good to connect. Camaraderie was instantaneous with this team, and already I had a good feeling about our upcoming mission. Teamwork is the key to success in small-team special operations. With Nate's team and mine excited to work together on a project the Department of Fish and Game was leading just a few days from now, our motivation increased significantly. We were both smiling when we shook hands before leaving.

On the long drive home I wasted no time and started making cell phone calls, confirming that Markos and Cheetah were free to work on the operation with my team. Still tense from the gunfight at Sierra Azul three years ago, I was relieved that we had a lot of levelheaded and skilled operators involved in this mission. I did not want to have to face another standoff with more gunmen, but if this did happen, I was confident given the makeup of our team. Within a few minutes the phone calls from Captain Huck and Chief Carmela were coming in, as well as eager calls from Markos and Cheetah. All the way home I pondered team logistics and the concerns I had for the mission that was just a few days away.

The day before the Fay Creek mission, after triple-checking my tactical gear and patrol truck, I left my house and started the long drive toward the Kern and Tulare County border. All of us involved would be meeting at the command post that afternoon for Nate's mission briefing. These briefings were the calm before the storm and a time when game wardens from far away got to meet and visit again after long periods of time apart. With about 200 of us in the field at any time to cover the entire state, we are spread out over great distances and seldom get to work with others outside our squad. Because we share so many goals and experiences, and we work alone so much, Fish and Game wardens become like family members, and we all look forward to seeing each other but rarely get to do so. This briefing was a time not only for us to understand all aspects of the operation and each person's role in it but to also renew bonds and visit with distant friends.

The energy during the briefing was already in high gear. This was a new type of takedown for our enforcement staff, and it would be precedent setting. While I knew that many of us in the warden ranks involved in this operation were from different divisions, until I walked into the room I did not fully realize the level of involvement of our entire department. This was big. Alpha, my long time friend and the lieutenant and her wardens from the Department of Fish and Game's Special Operations Unit, the department's covert squad, were all present. That team had worked surveillance on this case for countless hours, helping establish which felons outside the cultivation site in the woods were involved in this network and how far outside the central valley it reached. Alpha and I had taught a wildlife investigations class together in Cambodia for the Department of Fish and Game two years ago, and we enjoyed working together and did so effectively. It was always great to see her and work with her team.

Also present was John, another lieutenant and longtime teaching partner and friend. John is the team leader of the Delta Bay Enhanced Enforcement Program, an overt special operations team responsible for handling enforcement issues throughout the Sacramento Delta region of California. He and I have worked together and taught firearms and defensive tactics classes for several years at both the Fish and Game and other police cadet academies, and his firearms knowledge and proficiency, coupled with his team's tactical skills in the field of high-risk warrant entry, made his team ideal for handling the early morning search and arrest warrant entries on residences in the valley. And to no one's surprise, John's team would be handling the raids on homes in the suburbs while we were running the raids in the woods in a coordinated and carefully timed operation. I was feeling more confident and excited by the minute as I saw the personnel in the room and learned their specific missions. Nate had hit the bull's-eye with his selection of personnel.

The enforcement staff from the district and Nate's squad specifically was huge. Nate's wardens had tasks ranging from press briefings and equipment and personnel transport to handling the marijuana once removed from the grow site. The local squad members who developed and worked the case from its inception were mingling with officers from all over the state.

For those of us handling the special ops functions of the operation, the detail was broken down logistically in the following way. I was leading the first team on the ground for the arrest and eradica-

tion detail within the Canebrake grow site, while Connell was leading the second ground team. The third team on the ground was a
pair of game wardens positioned on a mountain top above us to
oversee the action in the garden below us, and guide us from above
when possible. Lt. John would be leading his Delta Bay Enforcement team on a high risk search and arrest warrant entry in the
suburbs of the city below, while another Lieutenant's squad would
be conducting a similar high risk arrest and search warrant entry in
another part of the city. Lt. Alpha would be overseeing her team of
covert operators, as they maintained surveillance on the suspects
and their residences throughout the city.

Again, I felt the energy of such a big operation underway and
marveled at how many parts it took to make this mission whole
and successful. I made the rounds greeting Nate's guys and the rest
of my colleagues before connecting with Fish and Game's Chief of
Patrol.

Chief Foley, with her trademark calm and quiet demeanor, was
smiling as the operation came together. Nancy is the first female chief
of the department's Law Enforcement Division and she always makes
it a point to be in the field with her wardens when major operations
like this one take place. She asked me how the operation was going
on my end, and I told her the good news. Our teams were solid, we
had a good plan, and our support system, in addition to the operators
on the ground, was second to none. She was pleased. I could tell she
was as excited as the rest of us. Always supportive of our catching bad
guys and a game warden at heart, (she had previously been head of
Fish and Game's Special Operations Unit), Chief Foley would be staying overnight to see the operation through to the next day.

Another unique part of the next day's mission was the immediate environmental reclamation we would implement as part of the
overall operation. This was not going to just be an arrest and eradi-

cation detail. Because Canebrake is a property owned by Fish and Game, Nate had arranged to have the department's Environmental Science (ES) personnel from his district on scene to help assist enforcement staff with the immediate reclamation of the site. Once our teams cleared the grow site of all threats, arrested the growers within, and eradicated the plants, ES and enforcement staff would come in and reclaim and clean up the site together.

Nate's briefing went smoothly. Because most of us knew our tasks and had worked out logistics before the meeting, there were few questions following the overview. We were pleasantly surprised during the briefing to learn we would have helicopter support for this operation. With the help of the Kern County sheriff's office Jet Ranger helicopter, all the irrigation pipes, camp trash, fertilizers, and other pollutants would be removed and disposed of *that day,* a rarity in marijuana eradication protocol throughout the state due to time constraints and lack of funds.

The Jet Ranger was similar to the CAMP choppers and could haul out eradicated marijuana plants, short-haul officers as needed, and, heaven forbid if it should happen, drop in medical support to an injured officer. Prior to the briefing, Nate and I had discussed the lessons learned in my county when Mojo was shot in 2005. My team all remembered that unacceptable three-hour delay and the debacle trying to get air support to aid and extract our critically injured officer. We vowed that we would *never* let that happen again.

Following the meeting, Connell and I gathered our teams and started the drive south to Lake Isabella. We needed to see the environment we would be working in. All of us on the field team spent the next two hours convoying down to Lake Isabella before getting our patrol trucks parked and stored at the hotel. After stowing our gear and getting some covert vehicles sorted out for an evening site survey, we headed for the Canebrake Ecological Reserve.

Markos, Cheetah, Will, Connell, and I all packed into a van, left the hotel, and headed north to see the starting point of the next day's operation. When approaching the eastern border of the ecological reserve, the beauty of the terrain struck me immediately. Strikingly different from the oak and brush woodlands we were used to operating in back home, this high desert terrain consisted of steep hills covered in large boulders, high grasses, pine trees at mid-elevation, and random spreads of heavy brush.

The terrain here had the same tactical challenges as our operating fields back home. We would be loud on the dry ground this time of year; I now understood what Nate meant when he said remaining silent in the woods would be difficult. Regardless, working in this new and varied terrain added to the excitement of this operation and the uncertainty of what our teams would encounter in a few hours.

To avoid being detected, we spent just enough time driving by the Canebrake border fence to decide where I wanted our team to start in the morning. Getting the teams dropped off without detection in the early morning darkness was critical, and timing, stealth, and efficiency would be everything. On the way back to town we discussed the fine points of getting so many operators dropped off and in the woods smoothly the following morning.

Once back in town we enjoyed some dinner with Connell's team. Then it was time to get our gear prepped for the operation and a few hours' sleep. Talk among both team members in our hotel parking lot was lighthearted and enthusiastic as we checked our weapons, tactical gear, and other mission essentials. Go time was less than six hours away, and we were getting pumped.

I was lying awake in my rickety, lumpy hotel bed for thirty minutes before the alarm went off. During those thirty minutes I thought about every possible aspect of the day's operation that I needed to focus on to make our teams effective and keep them safe. Four o'clock came and it was time to roll. We were ready with a good plan. It was time to get it done.

By 4:30, under a star-filled desert sky, our teams completed their last equipment checks and were in a convoy of dark patrol trucks rolling north from Lake Isabella. At 5:00 a.m. we were at a staging area to drop off some of those trucks and trim the convoy to only a handful of vehicles. We needed to get to and away from the dropoff point with as few vehicles as possible and do so quickly to avoid detection. Once at the dropoff point it was critical to get our teams over the reserve's border fence quickly and away from the road. Once clear of the fence and at a short distance into the property, two large teams of camouflage-clad operators could blend into the rocky and brushy desert country near Fay Creek.

Close to 6:00 a.m. we were out of the trucks and double-timing it to the fence. With Adam and Markos on point covering ahead of the team, I crossed the fence, with the rest of Team 1 following behind. A little farther down the road, Team 2 was being dropped off and making its entry into the reserve as well.

With the predawn sunrise just starting to illuminate the desert terrain around us, Adam and Markos led our team across the flat desert valley at a moderate pace. With no need or reason to stalk quietly at this point, we moved as smoothly as possible to get off that open valley before the sun crested the eastern foothills and exposed us.

We made good time across the flat, maintaining a low profile. We stopped when we reached the edge of a dry tributary to Fay Creek. With the team staged and our point guys and tail gunner covering our rear, I called Connell on the radio to check on his team's progress. Connell responded that his team was across the fence and cutting across the valley not far behind us. This was excellent news, as they were right on schedule.

Moving silently through the brush and dry leaves near the dry creek drainage was impossible, and no matter how slow and carefully the team progressed, we still made more noise than I was comfortable with. Realizing this, I approached Adam and Markos and discussed the situation in a quiet whisper. Using his knowledge of the area, Adam made a good suggestion and Markos and I were in agreement. We were less than a half mile from the first of the two gardens now and had to bring our team in to stalk the growers from another direction to be effective. Working in from the east at a straight diagonal before descending on the grow site this close to the garden as planned was likely to compromise our team. It would surely eliminate any chance of making some arrests today.

It was decided that Adam and Markos would turn the team north and upstream along the dry tributary to get us farther away from the garden. By doing so, we could make a little more noise without risking detection and put the team in a better location to descend on the grow under quieter conditions. We moved smoothly upstream now, and once across the dry channel, we found ourselves standing on a sandy-based grassy hillside, with several smooth game trails all around us. With quieter conditions, we were in much better shape to stalk the felons effectively.

Another radio check to Connell brought good news. His team was staged at the base of the dry creek drainage, not far from the grow site and standing by to move when we needed them to. Connell and his teammates had done a great job of getting through some noisy terrain undetected and were posted less than a quarter of a mile from the garden. They were so close in fact that they could actually hear the voices of the growers tending their cash crop.

And just when I thought it could not get any better, I got a radio call from Terry and Scott from their observation post on a rocky and brush-covered hill about 500 feet tall located southwest of the first marijuana grow. Unlike any other arrest eradication mission I have participated in, this terrain had the added benefit of a valuable third team for the arrest and eradication part of the operation.

Given its strategic location and with all the characteristics of a sniper's ideal hiding spot, the observation post on the hill was a perfect place to monitor movement in the grow site. Using binoculars and spotting scopes, Terry and Scott could monitor the grower's locations, their movement, as well as the location and progress of our teams. And most importantly, the observer team could let me know on the ground when the bad guys were getting close. What a great asset those guys were!

Terry told me he had his eyes on two growers' backs as they bent over tending their plants in the center of the garden. While he could not see my team yet, he knew from my description of the drainage we just crossed where we were approaching from and generally how far away from the grow we were. Terry could not yet see Connell's team because of the drainage they were concealed in, but he also knew roughly where they were located in relation to the garden. Terry knew his guys were close to the grow, and with the noisy terrain around them, he suggested they not move into the grow yet. Doing so would surely push the growers to flee, and my team was too far away to be able to catch them in a bottleneck.

I acknowledged this, thanked Terry, and called Connell on the radio as we worked toward the garden slowly, making sure the area was clear of anything threatening along the way. Responding as quietly as possible, I knew his team must also have been close to the garden since I could barely make out Connell's whispered response.

He would keep his team stationary and concealed in the drainage until he heard from me.

With my team ready to move, I relayed the message to move out up to Adam and Markos who were on point. I patted Cheetah on the shoulder and whispered to him to be ready for his chase. He and José both looked back and smiled, eager and ready to put the grab on some bad guys.

We continued moving quietly down the sandy wash until we reached a T intersection with a well-worn foot trail just ahead of us. Two sets of fresh tennis shoe prints going in both directions on the trail validated what we thought. Two growers were using this trail a lot. And while we all knew the prints to our left and to the east led to the garden, we were unsure where the tracks going to our right and west led to. Perhaps another garden or the grower's camp made the most sense, but we would not know until we got there.

Since we knew there were two growers working in the garden, I decided to move the team west and follow those tracks. I did not want to be ambushed by more growers coming from behind us on that trail if we were stalking into the garden from the same direction.

After covering less than 100 yards, Adam and Markos could see a tent hidden in the brush up ahead. Instantly both point operators gave the closed-fist hand signal and stopped the team. I radioed to our point and running teams and together the five of us advanced slowly on the tent. When close enough to the tent and from positions of concealment, Markos and Adam identified our team and challenged anyone who might be inside as quietly as possible. After several announcements and no response, Markos and Adam advanced on the nylon sleeping quarters and quickly breached the front zippered door before entering the tent and giving the all clear. No one was inside, and from the looks of it, this was clearly the camp for the two growers who were working the garden. Two sleeping bags and additional clothes and boots for two men confirmed the story.

Underneath one of the sleeping bags, Markos found a .45 ACP caliber pistol magazine filled to capacity with .45 ACP ammunition. When examining the magazine myself, I could see it was meant for a Firestar .45 automatic pistol, a high-quality Spanish handgun known for its reliability.

Another sweep of the tent did not uncover the handgun that went with this magazine. That meant one thing: one of the growers in the garden most likely had the pistol on him. This .45 caliber pistol is a potent antipersonnel weapon, designed to kill people, and is used by law enforcement and the military in certain parts of the world. It was clearly being carried by a grower for one reason and one reason only; to threaten, harm, or kill intruders.

Suspecting that we were dealing with armed growers, I got on the radio and told all three teams that one of the growers might be armed. Connell had to know right away that less than a few hundred yards ahead of his team at least one gunman in the garden had an automatic combat pistol in his possession.

Retaining the pistol magazine as evidence, our team left the tent and turned around to begin following the trail in the opposite direction. Now moving toward the garden and the growers in it, I cautioned everyone to be on high alert and ready to freeze and find concealment instantly in the event the growers left the grow and walked back to camp.

Once our team advanced about 100 yards toward the grow, Terry told me he could see us moving along the trail sporadically in between the pine trees surrounding the footpath. Just as he was describing how far away from the garden we were, he suddenly changed his tone and said frantically, "Team 1, the growers are on the move! They are out of the garden and headed your way on the trail! And they are moving fast and getting close, less than 200 yards now!" Terry and Scott high above us were watching the entire operation play out three dimensionally like a real-life war game. Watching the two forces converge from that distance must have been surreal, and the excitement and emotion in Terry's voice on the radio gave me the chills and an instant adrenaline dump before I relayed the information to my team.

"Copy that Terry!" I whispered instantly. Before I could tell the rest of the team to get off the trail and find some good cover to hide in, Markos and Adam were already ahead of the game. Our point men were rapidly moving the team off the trail in a double-time run. They had found several truck-size boulders, a gift from above, all around the trail to hide the team. These boulders could not have been more conveniently placed for us to stage an ambush and catch these felons as they moved past this spot. How fortunate we were to have Terry and Scott as our eyes in the sky.

The team divided up, with half of us hiding behind one rock and the other half hiding behind another. Once in position behind this excellent cover we waited. I whispered to Terry on the radio and asked for a sit-rep. I needed to know how close the growers were to us now. Unfortunately the tree cover was too thick for him to see the growers or us, and it was up to our team on the ground to handle this one for now.

Within the next minute the two men appeared on the trail ahead of us. Both were moving quickly, talking quietly, and one of them was carrying a pistol-gripped shotgun. As they passed our position, all of us behind the rock moved slowly around it counter-clockwise mimicking their rate of speed. As we rotated around the boulders, everyone remained out of their view and slowly ended up behind the growers whose backs were turned as they passed us completely. I did not have to say a word and knew what was coming next. As soon as Adam, Markos, Cheetah, and José made it around their boulders and the men passed, the chase would be on.

And then everything exploded. All of us up front were yelling and identifying ourselves and directing the men to stop and comply with their hands up as both growers broke out in a run to get away. One of the men threw the shotgun down on the ground as he turned to start his run, apparently wanting nothing to do with that type of fight. Before the growers completed their turns, I saw Cheetah and José take off like lightning, running at a full sprint toward the felons. Like the rest of us, Cheetah and José had no faith in the men simply giving up so we could arrest them.

As Cheetah and José chased the men through a small drainage next to the trail, Markos, Adam, and I followed as quickly as we could with our patrol rifles and big packs. José was in the lead with Cheetah right on his tail, and they were gaining on both men quickly. Within 50 yards, José and Cheetah had tackled the first man along the bank of the dry creek drainage.

As if running a relay race and handing off the baton to the next runner, José jumped up and sprinted toward the second man. Cheetah had already started to handcuff and search the first grower as Markos arrived to support his partner with his M14 rifle. Markos covered the fleeing felon as Cheetah finished handcuffing and searching the suspect, now under complete control and no longer a threat to the team.

Seconds later, José had tackled the second grower halfway up the steep bank of the creek drainage below. Like Markos, Adam was right behind José, covering his fellow operator with his AR15 rifle as José handcuffed and secured the man.

The chase had lasted only a few seconds, and everyone had acted intuitively and performed well when the chaos started. I was so impressed to see two running teams of officers from three different agencies who had not worked together before work so smoothly together that morning. This was the first time we had used running teams to effectively chase down and catch *two* growers, and it could not have been on a better operation where our department had such a big stake and such responsibility in this mission. I let out a deep sigh of relief that we had these two men safely in custody and that they had not used any guns on us.

Within a minute, Connell's team reached the drainage to support the chase. Seeing his team appear at the top of the hill above us gave me a real feeling of relief yet again. Our teams were now safely together with two bad guys apprehended and everyone in great spirits. Connell looked down and asked if we were okay. I looked up and smiled, giving him a thumbs-up and saying, "Thing's are more than okay, buddy. We just scored 100 percent today! We got both growers in a short chase and have a gun or two to collect on the trail behind us!"

With the two growers in custody and detained by Cheetah and José, Markos and I backtracked the foot trail to find the weapon. Within minutes, I found the shotgun on the ground next to the trail. It was a Mossberg Model 500 pump-action 12 gauge with an extended magazine, and it was loaded with seven 12-gauge shells with one in the firing chamber. Markos and I immediately noticed the gun's trigger guard was missing, leaving the trigger exposed just forward of the shotgun's pistol grip. This made the gun completely unsafe. Without the trigger guard, the weapon could have discharged unintentionally during the chase. This could have led to a gunfight and maybe one of my team members' being injured or worse. Again, I was thankful.

I cleared the firing chamber of the 12 gauge and unloaded the rest of the shells from the magazine as Markos continued down the trail searching for additional weapons. Within a few seconds he called, "I think I found the other half of that pistol magazine!" With that said, Markos bent over on the trail and picked up a Firestar .45 ACP caliber automatic pistol, a match for the loaded magazine we found inside the tent. Like the shotgun-wielding gunman, the second grower had thrown this pistol on the ground during the chase. Not surprisingly, the serial number on the handgun had been filed off, making it untraceable and another felony violation. I was again reminded of how close we could have come to a gunfight and was again thankful it had not come to that.

Markos found the pistol loaded with a live round in the chamber and a full magazine. These guys were ready to shoot. Once both weapons were unloaded and secured, we hiked back to the rest of the team standing guard over the two felons. Connell asked me if we had things under control so he could move his team back to the grow site to begin eradicating. I told him we were in good shape, would be hiking the growers out of the garden for transport to jail shortly, and thanked him for all the support and a job well done that morning.

With members of both teams starting to assess the grow site and eradicate plants, Cheetah, José, and I escorted our two prisoners out of the ecological reserve. Both growers were subdued on the hike out of the grow site. Within an hour we had reached the border fence of the property. Seeing a Fish and Game patrol truck and two game wardens waiting for us at the fence line was a welcome sign. They were our relief and transport team. After I gave them a quick sit-rep on the morning's events, they took custody of both men and transported them out of the mountains and into town for booking and processing in the county jail.

Prisoner-free now, we needed to get back into the grow site and start assisting on the eradication and reclamation of the operation. Within thirty minutes, we had hiked back into the garden, and I was pleased to see that already it was almost completely eradicated. Connell's team and most of mine had been extracted from that garden and choppered into a second grow site discovered in another part of the reserve while Cheetah and I were hiking back to the first garden. Wardens from different teams were left in the first grow site to finish the eradication and assist in the reclamation and cleanup phase, and I jumped in to help.

On the hillside above me, I found Terry and Scott in the center of the grow stacking marijuana plants. Both officers were placing the big plants, some as tall as ten feet, on a cinch line used to wrap around large stacks of cut down marijuana plants to get them ready for helicopter extraction. Now off the hill and free from their observation-post duties earlier, they had hiked in to help the eradication and cleanup effort as well. Terry and I were all smiles when we greeted each other and reviewed that morning's events.

After getting the last load ready for extraction, I heard branches crashing in the creek bottom below at the southern edge of the grow. I hoped it was more department staff hiking through the creek to the garden and waited to see who it was. I smiled when I saw the familiar face of Chief Foley climbing over the last boulder in the creek to reach the garden. She had hiked in with Nate to lend a hand during the eradication. Once again I was proud of our department when I saw the leader of our enforcement division hiking into a grow site's ground zero to help her officers.

I greeted Chief Foley and as Nate joined us, she asked how the operation was progressing and how our ground teams had performed. We spent the next thirty minutes examining the growers' kitchen on the lower banks of Fay Creek and all the pollutants and trash poisoning the pristine watercourse right in front of us. Fortunately for this operation, that water-quality destruction was going to be stopped. And along with the rest of the grow site, this creek would be reclaimed and restored in just a matter of hours.

Chief Foley and Nate spent the next few hours working with the rest of us in the garden bagging trash, collecting and bundling up miles of black plastic irrigation pipe, and doing general cleanup to prepare the site for the restoration phase. The department's ES staff was on the way to take over where we left off. That group would be restoring vegetation on the stripped and exposed hillside above Fay Creek where all the marijuana plants had been cultivated. This would stabilize the hillside and prevent siltation and dirt erosion from entering and polluting Fay Creek once the winter months and rain set in. By next spring, it would be more difficult to tell this was a marijuana cultivation site, and it would look more natural and beautiful, as an ecological reserve should.

While placing several bundles of black irrigation hose in the helicopter net, I saw that John and several of the officers from his Sacramento Delta team had joined us. Early that morning John's team had executed one of two high-risk entries and served one of two search warrants on a residence belonging to members of the criminal network related to this cultivation operation. After entering the house with their search warrant, John's team found some great evidence. The second wardens' team had also done well when serving their warrants. Between the two search warrant teams, the department seized nine and a half pounds of processed marijuana, $6,900 in cash, one rifle, and two vehicles used in the conspiracy.

We finished loading a net with cultivation trash, and while we waited for the helicopter to return to extract this load, John and I took a break to discuss our team's performances earlier that morning. While we both felt our teams had done well, we knew there were fine points that needed improvement. Operations like this one show team leaders and trainers where to focus their training efforts, allowing us to not only improve the team's overall performance but add to officer safety as well. It was good to have a minute to discuss this with John. The day had been nonstop for both of us, and since the operation was winding down now we savored our minute to breathe and visit.

Once the last helicopter load of cultivation waste was extracted from the grow site, the rest of the enforcement teams left the garden once and for all. I hiked back with Chief Foley and Nate to the reserve border fence line and caught a ride with one of the many patrol trucks going back to the staging area to meet the rest of my team and pick up my truck. Markos and Cheetah arrived at the staging area about the same time I did. They had eradicated several thousand plants at the second garden and had an enjoyable helicopter ride into and out of that grow site while I was working in the first garden.

Between the two gardens on the Canebrake Ecological Reserve, our teams had eradicated 4,100 plants that morning. The cultivation sites caused significant disturbance and damage to the natural habitat along Fay Creek, including stream bank alteration, removal of riparian vegetation and other habitat features, and removal of water from the stream via irrigation pipes. The sites also contaminated the stream and surrounding habitat with pesticides, fertilizer, trash, and human waste. The illegal alteration of Fay Creek is a violation of the California Fish and Game Code, and in addition to cultivation and weapons charges, the pollution and littering violations were also important. As a result, the two gun-toting growers who were already in jail would later be charged with all of these resource-related crimes and be ordered to pay several thousand dollars in fines and spend several years in jail.

Once settled at the staging area, we unloaded and secured our rifles, peeled off our packs and other tactical gear, and changed out of our dirty and sweaty BDUs before checking in with the command post. Nate was busy coordinating the restoration of the grow sites, so our debriefing would have to wait until later when we could talk on the phone. After saying our good-byes to the chief and several of the district officers working around the command post, Markos, Cheetah, and I got in our trucks and drove into the town of Lake Isabella.

Over lunch the three of us discussed the excitement of the mission and how our team had handled the challenges of the day. I thanked Markos and Cheetah for doing such a great job throughout the operation, especially given the dangerous and challenging nature of their assignments. They were happy to have been a part of this mission, and we were all pleased with how well all the teams involved had performed. And more than anything, we were proud of our department and the professionalism it displayed throughout the entire mission.

Exhausted, we finished eating and left Lake Isabella to start our long drives home. My department was just getting into the peak eradication season, and I knew we would be busy for the next six weeks. That day, though, we would not worry about the hectic schedule ahead and would instead appreciate our teams and how much more effective we are when working together on these larger operations that need so much more personnel. My teammates would all relax and reflect on this mission over the next six hours on the long drive home. A new precedent had been set, and that felt especially good.

CHAPTER 7

Sanborn Park: Imminent Danger Close to a Kids' Camp

People sleep peaceably in their beds at night only because rough men stand ready to do violence on their behalf.

—George Orwell

It's 5:30 a.m. and I'm driving north on California 101. As I sip from my tall Starbucks, the rolling hills east of the freeway slowly materialize in the predawn twilight. Patrol dog Jordan is in the backseat, stretched out and dozing during the hour-long drive ahead of us.

This morning is the start of the 2009 season, and like the rest of the MET, I'm excited to be back in the woods stalking growers, destroying their illicit cash crop, and ending their environmental destruction. I'm also a bit anxious, and somewhat tired from having slept very little last night.

The first operation of the year is always a special one for the MET, with many of us working together for the first time since the previous summer. Team members constantly train to maintain operational status, but until we actually get back in the woods and start working together again—reading each other's movements, hand signals, and silent looks—none of us are fully *back in it*. Finding that comfort zone to successfully stalk and operate in the woods takes mission time, and this only comes from working with the same team members on a constant basis. When all is going well, we move as a coordinated whole, like a wolf pack.

Starting this season is even more exciting than previous years given the intensity of the events of 2008. As Rush's song "The Weapon" begins playing on my iPod, the first line of the song hits home immediately:

We've got nothin' to fear . . . but fear itself?
Not pain, not failure, not fatal tragedy?

I feel a chill thinking just how fitting it is for the mission we are about to begin.

Turning west onto Highway 85 toward the Saratoga foothills, I'm flooded with intense memories and images from the previous summer. The two-day CAMP operation in July comes to mind first and that exciting day Cheetah and I made that chase and suspect catch below Montebello Road, successfully testing the light running team concept for the first time.

Next is a flash of the joy of a successful chase just moments before I lost my footing and slipped with the big knife, making a deep cut into my leg. I saw my ragged flesh and blood-soaked BDU pants, and minutes later I left on an emergency short-haul ride back to my truck. I remember the big sigh of relief when I found out I could return with the rest of the team for the next day's mission above Saratoga.

Another memory flashes through my head as the imminent sunrise slowly illuminates the western foothills behind me. Those of us in the front of the stack on the point team were frozen silently on the quiet trail below Bohlman Road. Cheetah and I were ready to run as Snake and Ranger provided long gun cover on point while we all watched two armed growers moving through the budded marijuana plants. Suddenly another man popped out on the trail ahead, much closer than the other two, and started walking directly toward us. Learning just seconds later that this man was carrying a shotgun, had no intent of surrendering, and would fight us to the death, we engaged him with deadly force. The man's scream as he grabbed his chest instantly following the strike of Snake's well-placed shot echoes in my mind. I keep driving as another line from Rush's song hits its mark once again: ". . . And the things that we fear . . . are a weapon to be held against us."

I am reminded how quickly this work can turn deadly. Today's grow site is in the same area as that whirlwind two-day operation last year. Like any other mission, we will be focused and present for each other every second we are in the woods. Everyone must go home to their families tonight.

This is the earliest eradication mission we have ever conducted in our team's history. Unlike the hot and dry summer months when most of our operations take place, in late April our woods are covered in green grass and lush oak trees, and the creeks, springs, and ponds are full of water from the recent winter storms.

Most important for operational concerns, however, is the fact that this early in the growing season the marijuana plants are seldom more than a few inches tall. As a result, grow sites this time of year are relatively wide open with little vegetation to restrict visibility or movement. While this increased visibility is an advantage for our team, it is also more dangerous because there is less cover to conceal us. As a result, once our team reaches the outer perimeter of the garden, stalking and taking suspects into custody is much more difficult. This operation will test our stalking skills for the first time in a relatively wide-open grow site. There is no room for noise or any other errors today.

Because this site is located close to and has tributaries leading into Todd and Bonjetti Creeks, our team does not want to wait until harvesttime in late summer to eradicate this grow. We see no reason to wait for the plants to mature given all the environmental damage already occurring in and around the two watercourses. Even more alarming, however, is the fact that a children's outdoor science camp is located less than a half mile downstream from the grow site. With school in session and the camp currently being used for outdoor science projects and wildlife awareness, the area is full of kids enjoying the outdoors. All within a rifle shot of where this nefarious group of growers is cultivating its weed.

Pulling into the Sanborn Park parking lot thirty minutes later, I smile when I see the MET truck parked ahead of me. Huddled around it are a few of our team members talking among themselves. Their body language and facial expressions radiate excitement as the team prepares for the first operation of a new season. The eagerness to go back to work is obvious in everyone's demeanor, stronger than ever given the five-month hiatus since our last mission together.

I back my green patrol truck into the parking space next to the MET truck, and open the extra cab door to let Jordan out to join the team. Unlike scout missions where Jordan helps us with detection work, she will not be joining us in the field today. Instead she will stay back with the trucks at the trailhead, watching over our rally point for the duration of the mission.

Jordan's tail begins to wag back and forth at hyper speed showing how thrilled she is to be out of the truck and around the team.

Apache, childlike, starts to run and jump around with Jordan, eliciting happy and excited barks from her. After hugs and handshakes are exchanged among the team members, everyone gives Jordan some much appreciated attention. Over the last few years she has become a true four-legged member of the team and always makes us smile, even after the longest and most challenging days in the woods.

In addition to Snake, Apache, Ranger, Rails, and me, the MET has some new members joining the operation today. Miya is a young, tall, and agile operator from SERT, who besides having all the necessary skills, is also fluent in Spanish (always a great asset on arrest and eradication missions). He is a good fit for the team in all respects.

For today's mission, Miya is carrying his state-of-the art SERT building entry rifle system, a select-fire HK416 piston-driven carbine with an electronic red dot optic. This weapon has proven effective and reliable by U.S. Special Operations forces in the deserts of Iraq and Afghanistan, and we are encouraged to see it deployed in skilled hands for the first time on one of our team's operations. Adding good operators and quality weapon systems to the MET is always a benefit to the team.

Also fairly new to the team, Fordy has an extensive background in undercover work in several areas of special operations and is an expert in narcotics investigations on many levels. Like Miya, Fordy is always positive, helpful, motivated, and hard working. Besides being a good fit for the MET, he adores Jordan and always gives her positive attention when we are all together. Given that, what's not to like?

After a quick catchup session, we gather around the trucks to begin the mission briefing and go over the operational plan for the day. Jordan responds to the stay command and sits quietly next to my left foot as Apache starts to talk. Unlike previous seasons, Apache is now the number two member of the MET, assigned permanently to the team. Today is his first operation as team leader, and his voice relays his intensity and seriousness.

Apache starts by pointing out that this garden site is one we discovered at the very end of the 2008 season, but it had already been harvested and abandoned. Earlier this month a property owner contacted Apache and Snake, telling them a friend of his had been hiking the Bonjetti Creek channel and spotted a grower working near the garden site. Fortunately, the hiker was not seen by the grower and managed to get out of the area without being hurt.

Following that report, Apache, Snake, and other operators on the MET scouted the garden site to verify the grow location, determine if it was currently active, and, just as important, determine how many growers were present at the site. The reconnaissance team found the site to be active with at least one grower present. The team saw the grower working in the garden area and planting many marijuana plants during their recon. Once the grower started walking back to his camp, the team moved out of the garden area slowly and quietly, avoiding detection from anyone in the grow site.

Given the close proximity of the grow to the children's science camp, Apache and Snake knew we had to jump on this operation quickly and attempt to arrest and eradicate as soon as possible. The reconnaissance mission took place just four days ago, and we were not wasting any time.

Apache next stresses the probability, not the possibility, that we would find at least one suspect at the grow site today. He also points out that given the small size of the plants and wide-open hillsides where the man is likely to be working, stalking up to and catching him would be tricky.

"We will separate the team into two units today," he says as looks over the operations plan. "Team 1—me, Snake, Rails, and Trailblazer—are assigned as the point team entering the grow site from above. Team 1 will also be using a pair of light runners up front with two long gunners on point for support, working slowly east to the grow site through the heavy wooded cover surrounding it."

Apache assigns Rails and me as light runners for today's mission, an arrangement that he and I had discussed and worked out last night on the phone. Rails is in the best physical shape ever, and has been running extended distances and conditioning for this assignment over the past several months. Rails had told me he wanted to make a successful catch on a grower this season and was keyed up to be assigned as a runner today. Rails added that he had been enjoying the physical training to become faster in the woods and to gain stronger cardiovascular endurance for the demands of the assignment. I smile back at him and hold up my hand with my index and middle finger crossed, the sign of good luck. As usual, Apache and Snake would be up front on point navigating and providing critical cover for Rails and me in the running positions.

Apache, now referring to the color topographical map in the operations plan, continues with the next assignment. "Team 2—Ranger, Miya, and Fordy—will act as a blocking force, approaching from the bottom of the grow site and moving in from the east along Bonjetti Creek. Once Team 2 is posted up and stationary on the lower edge of the marijuana garden, Team 1 will begin our stalk into the grow from above. If any of us on the point team misses or spooks any growers on the approach, the growers have nowhere to run except directly into the waiting hands of Team 2, silently hidden along the bottom edge of the marijuana garden." Apache's plan is received with smiles and nods of agreement. We all know that given the terrain features and approach routes at this grow site, his plan is solid and gives us the best chance of catching any growers.

With the smaller team formations set up, we are in good shape to stalk quietly throughout the operation. Given the open-field conditions within the grow site and almost no concealment to hide our team's approach, stealth is a necessity with no room for errors once we get close.

After going over officer safety concerns, emergency contingency plans, and answering questions, Apache ends the briefing and we all disband and head toward our vehicles. I load Jordan in my patrol truck before driving out of the park and head north up Sanborn Road to the parking spot and the starting point for today's mission.

Under the cool canopy of trees in the parking area, Jordan will have to wait patiently in the back of the truck until the team returns and our mission is over. After a radio and equipment check and a careful and silent security check of all our vehicles, one by one the members of the MET slip silently through the rundown fence along the edge of the road and into the woods. Navigating slowly along the trail, I look back over my shoulder at my patrol truck and pause for a second to notice the look of disappointment in Jordan's eyes. While she is used to staying behind on some missions where it is too dangerous or impractical for her to participate, the sadness in her eyes is hard to take. Even at almost nine years old, her puppy-like spirit and energy level are high, and everyone can see her frustration in being left behind. I make a silent promise to my disappointed partner that following today's operation, I will take her on a trail run tonight for some time in the woods.

Both teams stay in formation along the trail for the first mile of the hike toward the grow site. The separation point for our two teams was ahead of us on the edge of Bonjetti Creek, and at the junction we all stop, and wait for a moment to just listen and let the woods settle around us. The woods are quiet with no sign of human presence anywhere. The grow site is less than a quarter mile ahead of both teams now, and stealth at every step is critical at this point.

Snake and I analyze his topographical map on the operations plan and talk over the routes into the grow site for both teams. "It looks like this is the best spot for our teams to separate," Snake whispers to me. Looking at the map, I nod in agreement as Snake adds, "Ranger's team has a shorter and quieter route to get into position than we do. If we give them a fifteen-minute head start, we should be getting into position a few minutes after them at this pace." Having Ranger's team silently in place before our team reached the top of the grow site gave us the maximum potential of surprising and catching any growers within.

I nod and reply, "Good call, Snake. If Team 2 can be hidden in position and set up a good ten minutes before we reach the grow site from above, we will have any suspects surrounded and are bound to make a catch." Snake folds his map and places it in his cargo pocket before telling Ranger the plan very quietly over the radio.

Seconds later, through our earpiece microphones we all hear Ranger respond, "Got it, Snake. Team 2 is ready and moving in one minute." Ranger will lead Team 2 up a trail and gradual hillside climb to the base of the grow site before stopping and waiting for our radio call. Our point team will have a steeper and longer hike to get to the top of the grow site and start our approach from above the garden, which means that we need more time than Team 2 to get into position. Besides the longer uphill climb, the thick brush piles along the way will slow us down as well. Unlike the stalkable grow sites from the 2008 season, this site has no clean and quiet trail going into it, making this stalk even more challenging.

After a last look at the map to verify our routes into the target area, our teams part ways and disappear into the vegetation. In the point position on Team 2, Ranger gives the hand signal for all three operators to move slowly off the trail and up the gradual hillside toward their objective. Seconds later, Snake signals our team to move forward, and just as slowly and quietly as Team 2, we move up the steep hillside toward the top of the garden.

The hike for our point team takes longer than expected given the noisy ground cover. While we all thought the soft ground and lush vegetation of spring would be somewhat quiet to move through, we are mistaken. The abundance of poison oak, blackberries, and every other kind of brush imaginable for that terrain is anything but quiet. The four of us on the point team take a solid hour to hike less than the quarter mile necessary to get to the top of the grow site.

When less than 50 yards from the edge of the grow site below us, we freeze, listen, and scan the woods ahead of us with our binoculars for any growers. After five minutes of seeing nothing move, Snake slowly gives us the hand signal to spread out in a skirmish line and begin a slow advance to the edge of the grow. This will allow us to see into more of the site once we make it to the perimeter line of brush and vegetation. With Rails and me in the middle of the line, and Apache and Snake covering both outside flanks, we advance deliberately one slow step at a time. Our Glock pistols out at the low ready, Rails and I move and scan slowly ahead, as Snake and Apache do the same to our left and right with their AR15 carbines.

The natural forest is separated from the cultivation crime scene below by the last of the tall brush and small trees just 10 yards ahead. We all know we will soon be looking over a cliff of brush and down into a stripped hillside full of small marijuana plants. One or more growers could be anywhere within a 200-yard line spanning north to south below us. We can only hope to get lucky and see our target suspects close to our position as we reach the edge of the brush line.

Rails and I stand silent next to several tall manzanita trees. Apache and Snake are also frozen in their positions around us and looking into the grow site ahead. All four of us see the same thing: black polypropylene water hoses leading to countless irrigation circles surrounding thousands of small marijuana plants. The grow site is so quiet that we can hear the water trickling through the water lines below. Only when I use my mini 8-power binoculars can I make out the pot plants. They are all no more than 4 inches tall and have clearly not been in the ground much longer than a few weeks. We have reached this garden at its infancy, almost a full four months before harvesttime.

Snake whispers into his radio microphone and receives a sit-rep from Ranger's team below us. Team 2 is now in position and has actually made it a lot closer to the grow site than planned without being detected. The operators are hidden in the brush and treeline below the grow site, just a few yards from the lower edge of the garden. If anyone is in the grow or in the camp area, one of our two teams will detect it and have the advantage of surprise and containment on both sides of the grow.

A rush of adrenaline sweeps through our unit as all four of us on the point team simultaneously see a man materialize from the southern edge of the grow site. The grower is about 25 yards away from us. He is well over 6 feet tall, and as expected, he is dressed in clothes that fit the terrain (brown T-shirt and dark jeans) and blend ideally with the surrounding vegetation. Looking nervously in all directions, he walks through the garden site, clearly unaware of our presence. This is a relief, given how close both our teams are and how noisy our approach proved to be.

Like frozen statues, the four of us watch him from above. The slightest movement from any of us will surely lead to detection. Without moving his head, Snake whispers our find to Ranger, and his reply tells us all that his team also has eyes on the suspect. They had detected the grower's movement when he left the camp area above the creek and began moving through the garden site toward our location a few minutes ago. Fortunately, both our teams were in place and not moving when the grower was on the move. While timing and coordination is always critical when stalking with two or more teams in the woods, today we are exceptionally lucky that everyone is exactly where he needs to be.

The grower eventually stops and turns around to face downhill in the direction of Team 2. As the man squats down on the ground next to several recently planted marijuana plants, we can see he is holding a bowl and eating some food from it with a small spoon. Between bites, he puts the bowl down on the ground before picking up a flowing water line to irrigate some of the numerous plants around him. This continues for several minutes as the four of us above him remain frozen.

Rails and I are especially stuck. The grower is less than 20 yards away from us at this point, with nothing between us except the thin line of small trees and brush separating the grow site from the woods. We will have to settle for moving as quietly as the terrain allows, realizing we will inevitably make some noise on our approach as we step through the maze of loud branches and brush below our feet.

With the perpetrator's back to us, Rails and I begin to slowly move forward through the brush line. I hope the flowing water in the grower's irrigation system will mask the sounds of our movement, and I hold my breath in anticipation as we slowly move toward our target.

We are advancing a foot at a time when suddenly the grower in front of us moves. Rails and I see this at exactly the same moment, and like two camouflaged statues in the brush, we stop moving and freeze again.

The grower stands up quickly from his squat and looks intently down the hillside in front of him to the east. Knowing Ranger and the rest of Team 2 are not far ahead of the man, I worry he has heard or spotted a team member below as he stares deliberately in that direction.

Like a deer watching a predator lurking in the brush, the man stands still and maintains his gaze downhill. The four of us on Team 1 freeze. An old special operations saying comes to my mind: We are not burned until we are burned. Assuming he saw us at this point is premature. Both teams wait, silent in the dark shadows and brush.

Seconds later, the grower's attention switches as he turns his head uphill and away from Team 2's location. His relaxed posture conveys to all of us watching that he is still unaware of Team 2's presence below him. When he puts the bowl of food in his left hand and begins watering more plants around him with the irrigation hose in his right hand, we breath a silent sigh of relief that we remain undetected. The grower is definitely nervous, though. Sensing this, Rails and I start to move through the brush to close the gap to our target while his back is to us. With Snake and Apache covering our movement with their optics and carbines, we once again advance slowly.

After only another couple of feet of forward progress, Rails and I have to freeze again. The grower suddenly spins his body around to face uphill in our direction. He stands frozen himself, gazing into the brush line, straining to see anything out of the ordinary. Less than 20 yards away, the man's dark eyes focus intently on our position. It is a standoff now, as our hearts begin to race.

We hope the grower will not see any of us and suddenly bolt toward the camp and escape. This is not the time to begin a chase. Given the brush line obstacle ahead and the gap between us and the felon, a pursuit at this point could end up in frustration. With none of our team members covering the camp to the south, and a labyrinth of heavily wooded creeks and escape trails in the canyon below, we could easily lose him. Like all other grow sites, this is his home, and his intimate familiarity with the terrain and how to escape it could lead to a futile pursuit.

The grower continues to gaze in the direction of our team above him for a good five minutes, and then, as if snapping out of a trance, he relaxes his stance once again and turns his head to the south. He now seems satisfied nothing dangerous lies ahead and begins walking toward the camp. We are not sure if the grower has a weapon, but he could easily have a pistol hidden in his waistband under his shirt, and before he has a chance to reach for it we need to act.

Using the noise and distractions of the grower's movement to mask our own, Rails and I advance quickly and carefully. The grower still has the bowl of food in his hands as he covers the ground with the long stride of a tall man. Completely clear now of the brush line above the garden, Rails and I are on the move. It is a wonderful feeling to be moving freely, even though it is not an all-out run like in past operations. Instead, we do a double-time stalk to be as quiet as possible as we gain on our suspect. We are quickly closing the gap.

As the hillside starts to curve around to the south toward the camp and creek bed below, the woods come alive directly ahead of the grower, stopping him in his tracks. Our suspect is now shocked and frozen in disbelief as Ranger, Miya, and Fordy rise up from behind rocks on the hillside just below the man's path on the trail.

Ranger is closest and materializes in front of the suspect when he stands up from the cover of his hiding spot. Now less than 5 feet from Ranger, and with the A2 flash-hider tip of Ranger's AR15 carbine barrel leveled at his torso, the grower realizes his day has suddenly gone to hell and starts to put his hands up. Petrified and shocked to see three darkly camouflaged operators with their rifles training on him, the grower loses any will to flee.

Ranger directs the man to put his hands up and lie down on the ground. He does so willingly, just as Rails and I reach the grower's location and the end of our pursuit. We work quickly to get the grower controlled further and holster our handguns before handcuffing and searching him.

We are not surprised to find a loaded Glock model 23 .40 caliber pistol in the man's waistband on his right side. Almost all the cultivation operations on this side of the valley have included firearms, and it's rare when we do not run across growers with long guns or handguns on their person or in their camps. Today is no exception, and like operations as recent as the one at the end of last season, we are fortunate to gain possession of the gun before he decides to use it. When removing the magazine from the pistol before unloading the weapon, I am again not surprised to see it loaded with hollow point ammunition similar to that used by law enforcement agents like us—ammunition used to stop people dead in their tracks.

As a result, this unlucky grower will be charged not only with cultivation of an illegal substance and environmental crimes related to pollution, littering, and streambed alteration but also possession of a firearm in the commission of a felony. This is proving not to be a good day for this man, whose array of serious charges will surely lead to a lot of time in jail.

With the grower now secure and a perimeter set around the camp area, our teams combine to get the eradication and environmental damage assessment and reclamation process under way. Before doing so, we conduct security sweeps throughout the entire grow site and post guards on our prisoner in the camp. As the rest of the MET begins working to eradicate the 7,000 tiny marijuana plants already starting to flourish along the hillside, I leave camp to investigate the full extent of the environmental damage associated with this grow operation.

The camp is full of trash, insecticides, fertilizers, human waste, and more pollutants, all on the banks and in the flowing waters of Bonjetti Creek. Just like my reaction to any other grow site this damaging, I am disgusted. I hike upstream a quarter mile to find the dam the growers built to impound water for their irrigation lines for the garden downstream.

The creek water above the dam is clean, clear, and cold, just like a high-mountain trout stream in California's Sierra Nevada. The surrounding ferns, grasses, and thick tree canopies above the creek are similarly pristine and beautiful. I pause for a few minutes to take in and reflect on the sound of the flowing stream next to me and the breeze through the multilayered tree canopy above.

Standing here I have a hard time imagining that more than a million people are hustling around the San José area only a short distance east of us, and yet these amazing natural areas are so close and provide so much to our environment and its wildlife species. I'm overwhelmed momentarily with the thought of the damage these growers are doing to so many areas not only throughout my county but throughout the rest of the state, and the nation for that matter, as well. And I'm disheartened when I think of the small number of operators in my agency and the handful of others fighting this violent war on environmental crime, a Thin Green Line of far too few to fix the problem on a significant level. I snap back into the moment and realize I need to get moving and help the rest of my teammates back at the grow site.

After taking evidence photographs, I remove the dam and irrigation lines from the creek. The fish and aquatic species thriving in this remote watercourse will now have a chance at survival. Restoring the natural and pristine flow of the channel to its natural condition feels good.

Back at the camp and with the help of my MET team, we remove the pollutants and trash either in, or in danger of washing into, the creek. After taking more photographs of the grow site and camp, all eradication tasks are complete, and it is time to leave and head for the trucks. Because it is so early in the season, and because we do not have helicopter support to short-haul us and transport our prisoner out of the woods, we will be hiking out with him in tow. For the next hour, we work our way back to the trucks, keeping careful eyes and hands on our prisoner along the way. He could always have friends hiding in the bushes waiting for an opportunity to free their comrade.

Fifty yards across the fence line up ahead of us I see Jordan's head pop up over the tailgate of my patrol truck. Having waited patiently for the last five hours, she has detected our approach and is excited to see all of us. With her tail wagging rapidly, her joy to have us back from the woods is obvious.

Such exuberant greetings from a very happy patrol dog soon have all of us smiling broadly. As we peel rifles and other tactical gear off our tired and sweaty bodies and grab cold bottles of water and Gatorade, we all reflect on the day. Our first mission of the season has been a success. As a result, Apache's debrief is short as he assesses the effectiveness and efficiency of our team. After saying my good-byes to the rest of the guys, and letting Jordan scam some affection from everyone one last time, we jump into my patrol truck and head toward the valley below to get home.

As we drive away I watch the rest of the team disappear slowly in my rearview mirror. I think about Snake and Apache in the MET truck, now chauffeuring the one man in our group who does not have a smile on his face as we leave the woods. I turn my iPod on and the Rush song takes up where it left off so many hours ago as I continue to drive down the windy road. I guide my patrol truck closer to home and the promised trail run with my pup, and I smile again.

My companion dog, Jordan, was diagnosed with terminal bone cancer two months following the Sanborn arrest and eradication mission. Because of her good health and strong body otherwise, she was able to continue working with me and the rest of the MET throughout the 2009 season.

In fact, in July 2009 Jordan was instrumental in detecting a large cultivation operation on one of the most difficult and challenging scouting hikes our team has ever completed above the Arroyo Hondo River watershed. As a result of that find, the MET eradicated more than 10,000 plants in that grow site alone and discovered one of the longest running and largest environmentally destructive grows above the sensitive waters of the Arroyo Hondo in the eastern foothills above the San José Valley.

As a result of her cancer treatment, Jordan had been operating effectively in the field on only three legs throughout the early spring months of 2010 when her illness had developed past the point of any further treatment. Her cancer aside, Jordan maintained a happy and loving spirit and continued to wait in the driveway every morning eager to jump into my patrol truck and go to work for two months following her amputation.

In early April Jordan's illness had taken its toll. Despite the eagerness and desire to be in the patrol truck and work in the woods, those gentle Labrador brown eyes told us it was time to stop. Jordan no longer had the strength to continue, and she worked her last patrol with her mom and dad before passing on April 15, 2010.

All of us on the MET honor and appreciate Jordan's contributions, energy, excitement, and the smiles and laughter she engendered in us countless times over the years. We have savored every day in the field with her, and every day of the nine and a half years she was with us was a blessing.

CHAPTER 8

Environmental Restoration and Prosecution: Taking Back Our Wildlands

A nation that destroys its soils destroys itself. Forests are the lungs of our land, purifying the air and giving fresh strength to our people.

—FRANKLIN DELANO ROOSEVELT

Besides the danger to public safety, one of the most important concerns of illegal marijuana cultivation operations on our public lands is the extreme environmental damage and wildlife resource destruction at most every grow site. And while not as exciting and action packed as chasing down and apprehending armed gunmen in the most remote areas of our forests, dealing with the egregious environmental crimes committed by these men is a major problem for resource-protecting agencies like the California Department of Fish and Game.

The pesticides, fertilizers, and human and general waste products used and produced by these men to grow their lucrative crops pollute and destroy natural waterways. Pristine creeks, springs, and wildlife and public drinking water sources for many miles throughout our forests are permanently scarred by these illegal grow sites.

In some cases an entire ecosystem of wildlife or a watershed is destroyed, and threatened and endangered wildlife species (such as red-legged frogs and steelhead trout), are killed for many miles along a waterway. From a Fish and Game enforcement standpoint, the pollution, streambed alteration, littering, and illegal poaching of wildlife occurring in these grow sites are significant problems that we have started to address on a statewide level. More game wardens are seeing the widespread and pervasive resource destruction these illicit gardens cause in our woods, and we all want it stopped.

Second only to the danger and safety threat these growers present to the public, trying to stop these environmental crimes from occurring and working to reclaim and environmentally restore these cultivation sites is now a mission of the Department of Fish and Game.

Unfortunately, this has not always been the case. When I started working eradication operations on a limited basis before 2004, environmental crime enforcement and cleaning up grow sites was unheard of, as was true of the Arroyo Hondo operation. In some parts of the state it still is. At the time, allied agency task forces had two goals in mind when raiding an illegal garden: destroy and/or remove all the plants, and if possible apprehend the growers responsible for their high-dollar crop. As a result, once an eradication operation was completed, the grow site was left with a bunch of dirt holes in the ground, sometimes miles of plastic irrigation pipe feeding those holes, and tons of trash and debris, not to mention large amounts of fertilizer, pesticides, paint, propane, and other polluting poisons throughout the garden, growers' camp, kitchen, and bathing areas. With a general lack of awareness of the environmental impact, however, and with cleanup *not* being a priority, these pollutants typically stay in the woods indefinitely. As a result, wildlife resource destruction continues long after the garden has been eradicated and the growers have left the area.

In 2004 my outlook on eradication operations changed drastically. The first chapter of this book describes the first large-scale cultivation operation I discovered in my district and the extreme environmental destruction to a pristine and remote watershed.

When I saw this I was disgusted beyond belief. To see so much damage from alteration, pollution, and poisons in one of the few quality steelhead trout watersheds in my district was disheartening.

After participating in that raid and realizing that without some input from a natural resource–oriented team member, environmental cleanup and restoration efforts on any level were not going to happen; it was not part of the agenda of our eradication team or its agency's command staff at the time. Not that they were unwilling or did not care, they were just unaware of this concept and did not have the manpower to easily take it on. Only with more game wardens working arrest and eradication missions and overseeing eradication teams through the clean up and environmental crime investigation process, will we be more effective in stopping this growing problem.

While it's important to be part of an eradication team, wardens need to do more than just cut down plants and chase bad guys around the woods. From our command staff at headquarters down to our individual squads, we hear it time and time again. In addition to arresting and eradicating, Fish and Game enforcement staff should be identifying the grow sites in *most* need of environmental reclamation and cleanup. Given time, manpower, and budget constraints, we cannot possibly reclaim and restore all the eradicated sites the team handles in a given growing season. Instead, we must assess the most sensitive sites with the highest damage levels and put our reclamation and cleanup efforts into those areas, including seeking the aid of other agencies and community volunteers. Even when our reclamation and restoration efforts are effective in one area, this does not stop growers from moving their operations to new and more remote growing areas to avoid law enforcement detection and ensure a successful harvest. But getting volunteers out to help with eradication also makes them more likely to report suspicious activity and makes them aware of who game wardens are and what they do.

The legalization of marijuana in California has been touted as a solution and a way to eliminate these environmentally destructive cultivation operations and the violence associated with them. Unfortunately, with the demand for marijuana in other states besides California where marijuana use will remain illegal, legalizing the plant in California is unfortunately unlikely to significantly reduce the amount of grow operations for profit throughout the state.

Just as our allied agency team does now on any eradication operation, wardens involved in eradication missions should be overseeing and implementing on-site restoration when possible on raid day. Even if a reclamation and restoration program is not possible at a later date, huge steps in protecting the environment can be taken during eradication itself. Once the garden is cleared of growers and made safe, wardens can work with allied agency team members to remove water diversions and impoundments and remove any trash or other debris in a stream that may be harming aquatic resources. This translates into longer work days for game wardens and allied agency officers working these operations, but if we wish to consistently reduce the amount of environmental crimes and damage throughout the state within these grow sites, this must become part of the job.

Our team practices this on every operation because we may not make it back to a particular grow site for reclamation and restoration for a long period of time, if at all. There is no better time to do this than when we have the most personnel available to spread out the work. On raid day eradications usually run smoothly and quickly because we have so many guys in the woods to help. And this applies to quick streambed repairs and hasty cleanup efforts to at least get the site through the winter without more resource damage from the grow. The way we see it, if wardens can help arrest growers and eradicate plants, then task force operators should certainly be able to help us do some quick environmental restoration on site.

Shortly following the shooting incident on Sierra Azul in 2005, I had a conversation with Snake regarding changing our role as a team when it came to eradication operations. I suggested that our MET start doing cleanup and restoration-oriented missions only during the off season when we are not doing arrest and eradication missions. Snake liked this idea and agreed. Especially given the fact that several game wardens are on the MET and help the sheriff's office with arrest and eradication goals throughout the county, he thought it only fair that they give back and assist my department with our environmental crime concerns.

As a result, Snake and I scheduled two cleanup days for mid-February 2006, well before the eradication season started. During those two days, the military's Pave Hawk helicopter and its crew assisted us in extracting large net loads of cultivation site waste products from each grow site. The big combat chopper has a huge payload capacity and can haul out thousands of pounds of waste cargo with each load. With the helicopter's capability to transport and dispose of those loads quickly at a centralized location, we would be able to remove a lot of waste and clean up and restore several grow sites in a limited amount of time. And with the marijuana from the grow sites previously eradicated, removed, and destroyed during the eradication phase of the operation, all our teams have to do now is focus on environmental clean up and site restoration.

Because of the flight crew's extremely limited availability, just having the chopper for a cleanup operation was a luxury. While we had worked with Team Hawk in the past on eradication and arrest missions, this was a first, and we were lucky to have the crew's help. Because the team had lately returned from rescue mission duties in Afghanistan and was slated to go back to the Middle East to continue supporting our fighting forces, we had caught the crew just in time for this mission.

Knowing this was not going to be a one-time operation, we were excited about starting this kind of program. I was particularly happy given my department's role in this arena. If the next two days were successful and this type of cleanup detail caught on throughout the rest of the state, the Department of Fish and Game could make some real progress in resource protection in cultivation gardens.

We included allied agencies and the press in this cleanup effort for efficiency and to educate the public and other agencies alike. The combined effort involved members of the Open Space Authority, the Santa Clara County Parks Department, and other resource-related groups. Staff members from all those organizations joined us and assisted us in bagging trash, removing creek diversions and water impoundments, and safely securing water polluting products days before Team Hawk's combat bird arrived to help us remove the grow site waste. Having established landing zones for cargo extraction and air support during those preflight cleanup days, we had eleven grow sites completely cleaned up and landing zones filled with a mountain of bags of trash ready for the Pave Hawk to hoist, remove, and dispose of when the detail started.

We started the cleanup effort on the site of the Sierra Azul shooting. Having operated in that garden only six months ago and knowing firsthand how much trash and pollutants needed to be removed, this was a good place to start. Snake and Rails brought other sheriff's office operators to assist the MET, and along with Mojo I had the help of several game wardens from my squad and some of the Fish and Game wardens who work the Santa Cruz coastline. We had a big team to get as much as possible done in a very short window of time.

After a deafening ride in the Pave Hawk to the edge of the shooting scene, we were all lowered into the grow site. We spent the next several hours restoring waterways, bagging trash, and hauling those bags to the landing zone where they were lifted out and disposed of. This continued for the rest of the day and into the next. By the end of the two-day operation, the MET had reclaimed, cleaned up, and restored eleven cultivation sites and removed over 100 tons of waste products from the woods. And that was over only a two-day period. It's amazing the amount of waste growers generate to make a cultivation operation work.

With members of the press on the scene, the environmental message sent throughout the San Francisco Bay Area on all the local television news channels that evening was positive. The public was alarmed at the level of environmental destruction in our woods, and few people had any idea that marijuana cultivation in our foothills was so dangerous, violent, and environmentally destructive.

This cleanup effort proved to be a success on many fronts and is now an annual program for our MET. Depending on the availability of air support with the military's Pave Hawk, we try to organize helicopter cleanup operations at least twice a year around the marijuana growing and eradication season.

Since our allied agency cleanup efforts started in 2005, task force teams throughout the state have caught on and are starting to appreciate game wardens and support our agency's mission as well. This is certainly evident in other parts of the state, including the large marijuana cultivation counties in central and northern California.

Another program we have implemented in our district involves volunteer groups to assist in cleanup and restoration. Environmental cleanup takes a lot of time and manpower, and the more people we can get into a grow site the better. The MET works with volunteers from state and local parks and recreation departments, Open Space Authority agencies, as well as Boy Scout groups and cadets from the Police Explorers Program in our district. This is a great project for environmental groups.

One of the most rewarding days of my career was our first cleanup day with a local Boy Scout troop and cadet explorers (pre-teen boys volunteering with a law enforcement agency to learn about it and later pursue a career in that field) working for the sheriff's office. We chose an eradicated grow site that was easy to get to on foot and made sure it was clear of any threat before bringing in our cleanup team. Also, before going into the site, I gave the boys a brief training talk on environmental crimes associated with cultivation operations, streambed alteration, and pollution issues.

When the boys reached the grow site, the disgusted looks on their faces said it all. These kids loved the outdoors and our wildlife resources and were upset to see so much environmental destruction in a cultivation site. For the rest of the day the scouts and explorers worked side by side with members of our MET and had the entire grow site cleaned up and restored by early afternoon.

With the press covering this cleanup detail and interviewing several of the boys for the evening news, the public message was clear. Like the rest of our society, our youth care deeply about our wildlife resources and want to see those resources remain intact for their children to enjoy.

Following the positive press coverage from our first cleanup operation, I received several calls from other volunteer groups offering to help our team on future details. The number of interested and impassioned people wishing to help was one of the most rewarding public responses I have experienced in eighteen years on the job. Our team's role in marijuana eradication has grown to include a public education and outreach element, and it feels great to pay it forward whenever possible.

❖

Historically when an eradication team is fortunate enough to catch growers in a grow site, the perpetrators have been charged only with crimes related to cultivation. Growers were typically charged and prosecuted for violations like cultivation for sale, use of a firearm while committing a felony, and other weapons and cultivation crimes. Yet, regardless of all the extremely damaging environmental crimes occurring in a cultivation site, these charges were seldom filed against the men caught in the garden. Like reclamation, cleanup, and environmental restoration, however, this situation has started to change for the better.

Since midsummer of 2006, our MET has been successfully collaborating with the Santa Clara County District Attorney's Office to get growers charged and prosecuted with Fish and Game crimes related to natural resources in addition to the cultivation and weapons charges. Now every grower we catch must answer for his wildlife crimes, as well as whatever else he is guilty of.

Our team's first environmental case against two growers we apprehended in a cultivation site was in July 2006. The grow was located in the Sulphur Creek drainage below Mount Hamilton in the east San José foothills and had been discovered by a backcountry trout fisherman. Realizing what he had hiked into, the angler was savvy enough to mark the location on his GPS before getting out of there undetected by the growers.

When assessing the grow site after our MET apprehended the two growers and secured the area, my discoveries were upsetting. Because this waterway is an annual flowing stream and serves as habitat for anadromous fish such as steelhead and native rainbow trout, the wildlife destruction caused by these two men was severe. Not only had Sulphur Creek been polluted and poisoned with pesticides and fertilizers from the grow site, but the typical water diversions, check dams, and pools dug out in the stream had changed the waterway's dynamics significantly. The growers had also killed a fawn near their tent, apparently using this baby deer for meat to eat. I was disgusted and had seen enough to write my report so that the district attorney could file environmental crime charges against these men.

The two growers were charged with illegal cultivation of marijuana, cultivation for sale of marijuana, and possession of firearms during the commission of a felony. Given that both men did not have any prior convictions, the harshest penalty the district attorney thought we could get was no more than one year in the county jail. When adding the charges for Fish and Game crimes, however, that changed. In addition to the cultivation and weapons possession charges just mentioned, the district attorney also charged the men with illegally altering a streambed without a permit, water pollution, littering within 150 feet of a state waterway, and the illegal taking and possession of a deer.

When it came time to go to trial, the growers wanted nothing to do with facing a jury of people who loved wildlife and hated poachers and polluters no matter what they were doing in the woods. Regardless of where individuals in the public sit on the marijuana cultivation issue, once a juror realizes that his or her drinking water is being poisoned and the wildlife in a watercourse has been destroyed for miles, we have all the support we need, and a conviction on a case this solid is a given.

Both men pleaded guilty to the cultivation, firearms possession, and environmental crime charges. As a result of the added Fish and Game crimes, the pair was sentenced to two years in prison, the first prison sentence any of our apprehended suspects had received up to that point. This was a significant victory for our MET and set a precedent on how we would continue to do business in the future when prosecuting more bad guys apprehended in grow sites.

The positive impacts the Department of Fish and Game has had on protecting wildlife by reclaiming and restoring environmentally damaged cultivation sites have been significant. With the help of allied agency task force officers, game wardens are saving and restoring our wildlife resources each and every time we participate in an arrest and eradication mission. With allied agency and public volunteer group support, the sky's the limit to what we can accomplish when it comes to grow site cleanup and environmental restoration programs.

With the ability to prosecute these resource criminals for wildlife crimes and convict and send them to prison for extended periods of time, we can keep some of the most damaging environmental violators out of the woods. This may not win the war against or completely stop resource destruction by marijuana cultivators, but it will at least slow these men from wreaking more havoc on our wildlife resources throughout this nation's wildlands.

The issue of marijuana cultivation and the importance of the statewide eradication effort are clouded with controversy. Some people do not view our efforts in this area as important or even necessary. In fact when people think of the war on drugs throughout the nation, marijuana cultivation falls at the bottom of the priority or awareness list. What the public has to realize is that members of these cartel groups cultivating within our state are willing to kill anyone who poses a threat to their crop. Any off-trails hiker, mountain biker, or equestrian is at risk of being shot if he or she stumbles upon a garden operation.

These illegal gardens are now widespread on remote public land tracts throughout California (and increasingly nationwide). We need to stop this proliferation and the associated environmental damages. For these reasons, this problem is a major issue for the Department of Fish and Game. We should be involved in removing not only these gardens that vastly destroy our state's wildlife resources, but also the growers who cause the damage and threaten outdoor recreationists as well. The Department of Fish and Game's involvement is not related to a war on drugs. It is instead a war on violence and environmental destruction—and it is our duty to stay in the fight.

AFTERWORD

by JAMES A. SWAN

To waste, to destroy, our natural resources, to skin and exhaust the land . . . will result in undermining in the days of our children the very prosperity which we ought by right to hand down to them.

—THEODORE ROOSEVELT

THE REAL SECRET SERVICE

The United States has more than 830,000 sworn local law enforcement officers, and 72,000 of them are New York City cops. In contrast, there are about 7,000 game wardens nationwide—about as many as the New York Police Department assigns to cover the city's New Year's Eve celebration.

State game wardens are known by various names—conservation officers, conservation police, game wardens, wildlife enforcement agents, fish wardens, environmental police, and fish and game wardens, just to name a few. Many are also deputy federal marshals.

U.S. Fish and Wildlife Service Special Agents—federal game wardens—are more rare than whooping cranes, with only about 240 for the entire United States.

No matter what you call them, game wardens have basically the same job: to protect our fish, wildlife, and natural resources by enforcing wildlife laws, and, as John Nores has made clear in this book, a lot more. Game wardens are community-based peace officers who have the largest jurisdiction of any state or local law enforcement officer—criminal law, civil law, traffic law, search and rescue, environmental education, and hunter education. They are a little like modern-day versions of the town sheriff in the days of the old West.

In California a Fish and Game warden must have at least two years of postsecondary education. After passing a rigorous exam, a warden must undergo sixteen months of training. About 60 percent fewer people applied to be wardens in 2006 than in the previous year, and 40 percent of those who enrolled in the last law enforcement academy left for other jobs, according to the California Fish and Game Wardens Association. Two of the most common reasons for resigning are low pay (game wardens earn about half what a California highway patrolman earns) and the dangers of the job.

Wardens are trained in wildlife law; report writing; firearms law; recognition of fishing, hunting, and trapping gear; arrest and defense tactics; patrol techniques; search and rescue; drug and narcotics enforcement; accident investigations; arrest techniques; first aid/CPR; interviewing and interrogation; emergency vehicle operation; crime scene investigation; the state's vehicle code, safety code, and penal code; weapons; weaponless defense; batons; and much more. This is tough training—a "high stress" academy, like boot camp. As many as half of the cadets drop out before completing their training.

If they choose to stay with it, game wardens work from a home office; are on duty 24/7; and patrol remote areas often alone and without backup in pickups, snowmobiles, planes, boats, ATVs, underwater with scuba gear, on horseback, trail bikes, and on foot. Game wardens also perform all their own crime scene investigations. Canine companions, like John's dog, Jordan, are increasingly popular as most wardens work alone in remote places and this is the only backup they get. Becoming a K-9 handler requires more training. Depending on the discipline, it takes a minimum of six weeks for detection and tracking and eight weeks for patrol, detection, and tracking. Then, there is ongoing monthly training after that consisting of sixteen hours for detection teams and twenty-four hours for dual purpose teams.

Most of the people wardens come into contact with are armed with guns or knives or both. Wardens' planes and trucks have been and are hit by gunfire. Wardens routinely contact and arrest armed convicted felons in remote areas with little or no backup. Ninety percent of public contacts on the job are nonviolent, but federal statistics show that game wardens and DEA agents have the highest risk of death on the job of all law enforcement agents. In the last century, at least 229 wildlife officers have been killed or have died in the line of duty nationwide. In California, game wardens are three times as likely to be killed in the line of duty as a California Highway Patrol officer.

All wardens are also Hunter Education Instructors; teaching people to use firearms, which is a dramatic departure from other law enforcement officers who discourage the use of firearms. The only other law enforcement officer who meets so many armed people in the field is a military policeman.

Little wonder that each California Fish and Game Warden is issued two .40 caliber pistols, a 12-gauge shotgun, and a .308 semi-automatic rifle, plus pepper spray and handcuffs, and a baton. They also train in "Defensive Tactics," otherwise known as martial arts.

Game wardens are not abundant anywhere, and as a result they are overlooked when people, including policy makers, consider law enforcement strength, funding priorities, and homeland security. The beat game wardens normally patrol is covered by few others wearing a badge—forest and park rangers, Border Patrol agents, the Coast Guard, etc. The scarcer that game wardens are, the less safe the woods, water, and natural resources, as well as the people who use them, are. Table 1 on p. 186, compiled with the assistance of the North American Wildlife Enforcement Officers Association, summarizes the numbers of game wardens across North America.

Table 1—Number of Game Wardens
In the Field, North America
February 2008

United States

Warden Numbers	Residents/Warden	Sq. Mi./Warden
Alabama		
139	33,086	365
Alaska		
96	6,980	5,958
Arizona		
86	71,701	1,321
Arkansas		
161	17,459	323
California		
192	192,000	795
Colorado		
135	34,000	764
Connecticut		
57	61,487	85
Delaware		
28	30,481	69
Florida		
722	25,055	75
Georgia		
211	44,378	274
Hawaii		
120	10,712	54
Idaho		
88	18,560	1,075
Illinois		
144	86,245	293

Warden Numbers	Residents/Warden	Sq. Mi./Warden
Indiana		
206	30,648	174
Iowa		
83	38,524	725
Kansas		
69	39,000	1,200
Kentucky		
157	26,790	25
Louisiana		
240	17,866	182
Maine		
124	10,658	249
Maryland		
238	23,595	41
Massachusetts		
100	64,371	78
Michigan		
141	71,600	403
Minnesota		
154	33,331	516
Mississippi		
165	35,153	417
Missouri		
167	34,986	412
Montana		
101	9,353	1,441
Nebraska		
60	29,472	1,281
Nevada		
31	77,897	3,567

Table 1—Number of Game Wardens (cont.)

Warden Numbers	Residents/Warden	Sq. Mi./Warden
New Hampshire		
42	31,307	214
New Jersey		
54	161,565	137
New Mexico		
67	27,149	1,630
New York		
264	73,128	178
North Carolina		
209	42,376	233
North Dakota		
35	18,169	1,970
Ohio		
88	130,431	465
Oklahoma		
118	30,332	582
Oregon		
119	31,099	807
Pennsylvania		
136	91,475	350
Rhode Island		
35	30,503	30
South Carolina		
261	16,557	115
South Dakota		
61	12,377	1,264
Tennessee		
181	33,364	255
(+ 95 part-time)		

Warden Numbers	Residents/Warden	Sq. Mi./Warden
Texas		
494	47,587	530
Utah		
65	39,232	1,264
Vermont		
40	15,000	240
Virginia		
150	50,953	264
Washington		
138	46,346	482
West Virginia		
126	15,542	206
Wisconsin		
151	35,521	360
Wyoming		
59	8,513	1,645
7,096		

Canada

Warden Numbers		Sq. Kilo/Warden
Alberta		
147	23,503	4,497
British Columbia		
137	31,927	6,895
Manitoba		
170	6,755	3,810
Nunavut		
34	882	61,764
New Brunswick		
101	7,423	722

Table 1—Number of Game Wardens (cont.)

Warden Numbers	Residents/Warden	Sq. Kilo/Warden
Newfoundland		
140	3,616	2,894
NW Territory		
63	677	21,367
Nova Scotia		
78	11,984	708
Ontario		
266	48,135	4,030
PEI		
8	17,328	710
Québec		
503	15,310	3,314
Saskatchewan		
197	10,309	3,309
Yukon Territory		
20	1,600	24,122
1,864		

California has 159,000 square miles of land, over 36 million people, 1,100 miles of coastline, about 222,000 square miles of ocean, 30,000 miles of rivers and streams, 4,800 lakes and reservoirs, 80 major rivers, deserts, mountains, urban areas, all of which are covered by game wardens.

California was admitted to the Union in 1850. Game wardens were the first sworn state police officers—more than fifty years before the California Highway Patrol was established. The first game wardens were deputy commissioners of the state's Fish Commission in 1871. A decade later, author Jack London switched from being an oyster poacher to becoming a game warden (then called the "fish patrol"), chasing down fish poachers in his sloop and writing a popular book about it called *Tales of the Fish Patrol*, in which he said, "Exciting times are the lot of the fish patrol: in its history more than one dead patrolman has marked defeats, and more often dead fishermen across their illegal nets have marked success."

By 1901 California had fifty game wardens, and the daily creel limit of trout and the daily bag limits for ducks and doves were also fifty. By 1907 the state warden force was expanded to seventy-three. In 1913 the first state fishing license was issued. It cost $1 for residents. The same year, two wardens were killed and three others were wounded in the line of duty. (Of the fourteen California Fish and Game Wardens who have died in the line of duty over the years, more than half were killed by gunfire.)

By 1949 California had 194 enforcement personnel, and in 1959 game wardens were granted full law enforcement status. However, they were not issued firearms and handcuffs until 1974. The warden force reached 280 in the field in 1998. Unfortunately, it has shrunk since, while other state law enforcement agencies have grown. The lack of public awareness of game wardens and understanding of what they really do are large factors in the warden shortage. As you well know by now, they do a lot more than check sportsmen's limits of fish and game, but that is what people associate them with.

About ten wardens are assigned to the Special Operations Unit that does undercover work primarily on felony conspiracy cases of commercializing wildlife. These guys and gals may work a case for a year or more, and they are some of the best character actors you will ever meet—posing as soccer moms, yuppies, surfer dudes, rednecks, and obsessed trophy seekers with great skill.

Because of the acute shortage of game wardens in California, in addition to the marijuana groves on public wildlands, a black market in fish and wildlife trafficking conservatively estimated to be worth more than $100 million a year is currently thriving and

involves the Mafia, the Russian mob, street gangs, drug manufacturers and users, and drug cartels.

Table 2—Number of California
Fish and Game Wardens

Year/Number of Field Wardens	Population of the State
1871/2	565,000
1907/73	2.3 million
1949/194	10.5 million
1975/207	19 million
1980/244	23.6 million
1990/273	29.7 million
2000/275	33.8 million
2003/231	(50 positions eliminated)
2007/200	38 million
2008/192	(Proposal to eliminate another 38 positions)
2009/200	(Proposal to cut warden force in half—fortunately it was rejected)

Many people assume the citations for wildlife law violations are
a slap on the wrist. For minor infractions the penalties are not significant, but in California, where organized crime groups have become
so involved in wildlife crime, penalties are increasingly steep as the
seriousness of the crime increases. When someone commits a crime
involving selling something illegal, it becomes felony conspiracy. A
suspect convicted of a felony conspiracy charge is subject to a maximum of three years in prison and a $20,000 to $40,000 fine. Confis-
cation of cars, computers, boats, motors, firearms, and gear; loss of
hunting/fishing licenses; and so forth are always possible.

During the two years I spent making the documentary, *Endangered Species: California Fish and Game Wardens*, I had a lot of time to talk with wardens around the state about the job. I've worked with law enforcement at the local, state, and federal levels, as a stress reduction teacher, a consultant on anti-terrorism, in community relations situations, and as a consultant on "difficult" prisoners. The range of hazards for members of the Thin Green Line seem like the largest of any group I've had the pleasure of working with.

All wardens work from home offices, which means that family and home are exposed, and they can be contacted by people 24/7. They normally patrol alone, without partners or back-up (except perhaps a dog), in areas where radio dispatch and cellphone service dead zones are routine.

While on patrol, they traverse uneven ground by foot—mud, water, rocks, mountains, desert sands, cliffs, and heavy vegetation, where they encounter poison oak, rattlesnakes, scorpions, mosquitoes, Lyme disease, and West Nile Virus, bears and mountain lions, and all kinds of weather. They also venture into the backcountry on horseback and snowmobiles to patrol as well as perform search and rescue. When they patrol on the water, including out to 200 miles offshore, they board other vessels at sea, leaping from boat to boat as swells sweep through. And, contrary to everything else you've read, they also patrol the busiest city streets and stores, often interacting with diverse ethnic communities.

Game wardens inspect and seize more guns than any other agency, and on patrol nearly everyone they meet has a gun or a knife, often both. They discover and recover many disguised and concealed weapons, while wearing bullet-resistant vests that do not stop bullets from rifles.

On their patrols, they may do extended surveillances in adverse topography for hours—lying in mud, hot and dry deserts, snow, etc., perhaps wearing cumbersome waders or other specialized protective clothing. There's little wonder that game wardens also tend to have problems with skin cancer from continuous exposure to sunlight.

Most people think that wardens only come into contact with hunters, anglers, and other outdoorsmen and women. In reality, you've seen how they come face to face with drug cartels. Other characters commonly met by California game wardens include street gangs, drug manufacturers, the Mafia, and other organized crime groups. The woods are a haven for people who don't want to have to deal with society, including people on the lam. Little wonder then that game wardens are more likely to be assaulted in their line of duty than any other law enforcement officer.

As if humans weren't enough of a challenge, game wardens also have to deal with bears, deer, mountain lions, coyotes, bobcats, and rattlesnakes, as well as skunks, raccoons in the attic, and rabid animals of all types. These close encounters may result in exposure to numerous zoonotic diseases (diseases that are transferable from animals to people), such as rabies, Rocky Mountain spotted fever, Lyme disease, typhus, tularemia, bubonic plague, giardiasis, and anthrax. All California Fish and Game wardens are required to carry a card alerting medical personnel to the possibility that they may have been exposed to any of these diseases.

The bottom line is that game wardens have been operating as if they were invisible or as counterparts to animal control officers for way too long. As a result, our natural resources and many outdoor recreational activities have been suffering. Given the many challenges and hardships that game wardens are faced with, what is truly amazing is that they love their job. Career game wardens have an extremely strong esprit de corps that empowers them to stand up for wildlife and people. Hopefully this book will open minds, and open doors to help the Thin Green Line get the respect and support that they so rightly deserve.

RESOURCES

RAT ON A RAT AND GET PAID

One way to give the wardens a hand is to report poaching and polluting. Each state and Canadian province has a twenty-four-hour hotline for reporting poachers and polluters. If you see someone committing a wildlife crime, report it. If your tip leads to an arrest you will get a reward up to $1,000. To find the hotline for your state or province, go to www.naweoa.org/mod .php?mod=userpage&menu=1500&page_id=15

TO LEARN MORE ABOUT CALIFORNIA FISH AND GAME WARDENS ORGANIZATIONS

California Fish and Game Wardens Association www.californiafish andgamewardens196.com/

North American Wildlife Enforcement Officers Association, the voice of game wardens around the world, www.naweoa.org/, and its informative magazine, *International Game Warden,* http://www .igwmagazine.com/

DVDS

Swan, James and Andrew. *Endangered Species: California Fish and Game Wardens,* sixty-six-minutes, narrated by Jameson Parker. Available from Snow Goose Productions, P.O. Box 2460, Mill Valley, CA 94942. Web site: www.jamesswan.com/snowgoose/ wardendoc.html

TELEVISION

Wild Justice, a documentary series on California's game wardens beginning in the Fall of 2010, for National Geographic Wild.

BOOKS

Terry Hodges—a twenty-eight-year veteran California game warden, Terry has published four extremely entertaining books—*Sabertooth, Tough Customers, Sworn to Protect, Predators*, all by T&C Books—filled with great stories about the art and science of being a game warden in California. http://www.gamewarden.net/

INDEX

the Medal of Valor from Governor Arnold Schwarzenegger for his life-saving efforts and leadership.

James A. Swan, PhD, taught at the Universities of Michigan, W. Washington State, Oregon, and Washington before becoming a senior columnist for ESPNOutdoors.com, the author and co-author of eight books about conservation (including two Book of the Month Club selections), an actor in eighteen feature films and three TV series, and a TV producer. In 2009 James produced a video documentary on California's game warden shortage, *Endangered Species: California Fish and Game Wardens.* His writing and research have received awards from the American Public Health Association, the California Assembly, the University of Maine, and Psi Chi psychology honorary.

ABOUT THE AUTHORS

Lt. John Nores Jr. is an eighteen-year veteran California Fish and Game Warden who serves as the point man for California Department of Fish and Game anti-marijuana actions in the North Coast District. From June 2005  to the present, Nores has been Patrol Supervisor for three counties in the Central Coast of California. He currently conducts covert and overt operations and tactical surveillance and special operations training related to wildlife crimes, with a special focus on marijuana eradication. Along with his squad, Nores currently conducts overt and covert special operations throughout his patrol district. Nores also conducts tactical surveillance and special operations training related to wildlife crimes in his department, with special focus on marijuana eradication and environmental restoration. Along with the rest of the Santa Clara County Marijuana Eradication Team, Nores has helped eradicate more than 600,000 marijuana plants throughout Santa Clara County since 2003. In 2008, Nores received